PATHWAYS

SECOND
EDITION

Reading, Writing, and Critical Thinking

LAURIE BLASS

MARI VARGO

Australia • Brazil • Mexico • Singapore • United Kingdom • United States

NATIONAL GEOGRAPHIC
L E A R N I N G

Pathways
Reading, Writing, and Critical Thinking
Split 4A, Second Edition

Laurie Blass and Mari Vargo

Publisher: Andrew Robinson

Executive Editor: Sean Bermingham

Development Editor: Christopher Street

Director of Global Marketing: Ian Martin

Product Marketing Manager: Tracy Bailie

Media Researcher: Leila Hishmeh

Senior IP Analyst: Alexandra Ricciardi

IP Project Manager: Carissa Poweleit

Senior Director of Production: Michael
    Burggren

Senior Production Controller: Tan Jin Hock

Manufacturing Planner: Mary Beth Hennebury

Art Director: Brenda Carmichael

Compositor: MPS North America LLC

Cover Photo: An explorer traverses a glacier
    cave in Gornergrat, Switzerland: © Robbie
    Shone/National Geographic Creative

For product information and technology assistance, contact us at
Cengage Learning Customer & Sales Support, cengage.com/contact

For permission to use material from this text or product,
submit all requests online at **cengage.com/permissions**
Further permissions questions can be emailed to
permissionrequest@cengage.com

Split 4A:
ISBN-13: 978-1-337-62333-9

Split 4A with Online Workbook:
ISBN-13: 978-1-337-62494-7

National Geographic Learning
20 Channel Center Street
Boston, MA 02210
USA

National Geographic Learning, a Cengage Learning Company, has a mission to bring the world to the classroom and the classroom to life. With our English language programs, students learn about their world by experiencing it. Through our partnerships with National Geographic and TED Talks, they develop the language and skills they need to be successful global citizens and leaders.

Locate your local office at **international.cengage.com/region**

Visit National Geographic Learning online at **NGL.Cengage.com/ELT**
Visit our corporate website at **www.cengage.com**

Printed in China

Print Number: 03 Print Year: 2019

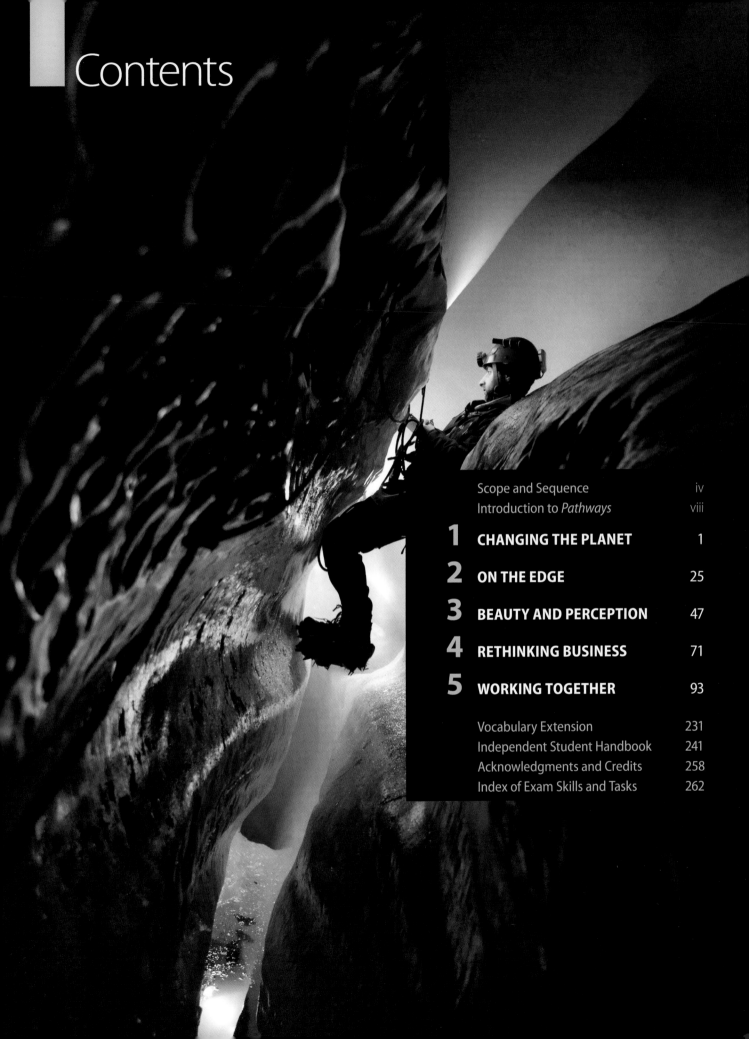

Contents

Scope and Sequence

Critical Thinking	Writing	Vocabulary Extension
Focus Analyzing Evidence Evaluating, Synthesizing, Guessing Meaning from Context	**Language for Writing** Using cohesive devices **Writing Skill** Reviewing essay writing **Writing Goal** Writing a cause-effect essay	**Word Forms** Adjectives ending in -ic **Word Partners** *dramatic* + noun
Focus Analyzing Text Organization Personalizing, Making Inferences, Synthesizing, Guessing Meaning from Context	**Language for Writing** Using appositives **Writing Skill** Reviewing the thesis statement **Writing Goal** Writing a persuasive essay	**Word Partners** Adjective/verb + *priority*
Focus Applying Ideas Inferring Meaning, Synthesizing, Guessing Meaning from Context	**Language for Writing** Using restrictive and nonrestrictive adjective clauses **Writing Skill** Supporting a thesis **Writing Goal** Writing an evaluative essay	**Word Forms** Nouns, verbs, adjectives, and adverbs
Focus Understanding Multi-word Units Understanding Visual Data, Inferring Meaning, Synthesizing	**Language for Writing** Using sentences with initial phrases **Writing Skill** Organizing a comparative essay **Writing Goal** Writing a comparative essay	**Word Web** Business words and antonyms **Word Forms** Adjectives with -ive
Focus Evaluating Sources Analyzing, Synthesizing, Guessing Meaning from Context	**Language for Writing** Avoiding plagiarism (I) — Paraphrasing **Writing Skill** Writing a summary **Writing Goal** Writing a summary essay	**Word Link** co-, com-, col-

Pathways Reading, Writing, and Critical Thinking, Second Edition uses National Geographic stories, photos, video, and infographics to bring the world to the classroom. Authentic, relevant content and carefully sequenced lessons engage learners while equipping them with the skills needed for academic success. Each level of the second edition features **NEW** and **UPDATED** content.

Academic skills are clearly ▶ labeled at the beginning of each unit.

NEW AND UPDATED ▶ reading passages incorporate a variety of text types, charts, and infographics to inform and inspire learners.

Explicit reading skill instruction ▶ includes main ideas, details, inference, prediction, note-taking, sequencing, and vocabulary development.

▼ **Critical thinking activities** are integrated throughout each unit, and help develop learner independence.

CRITICAL THINKING **Applying ideas** from a reading to other contexts can help you evaluate the information. For example, applying an author's opinion to your own experience can help you decide how far you agree with it.

ACADEMIC SKILLS

READING Understanding cohesion
WRITING Writing a cause-effect essay
GRAMMAR Using cohesive devices
CRITICAL THINKING Analyzing evidence

Reading

CHANGING FASHION
by Mike W. Peng

In the world of fast fashion, rather than only releasing a few new collections each year, companies like Zara sell a never-ending cycle of trend-led clothing, all year round.

Zara is now one of the world's hottest fashion chains. Founded in 1975, its parent company,[1] Inditex, has become a leading global apparel retailer. Since its initial public offering (IPO)[2] in 2001, Inditex, which owns eight fashion brands, has doubled the number of its stores. It has quadrupled its sales to US$25.7 billion, and its profits have risen to over US$3 billion. Zara contributes two-thirds of Inditex's total sales. In this intensely competitive industry...

Zara does not hail from Italy or France—it is from Spain. Even within Spain, Zara is not based in a cosmopolitan city like Barcelona or Madrid. Its headquarters are in Arteixo, a town of only 25,000 people in a remote corner of northwestern Spain. Yet Zara is active not only throughout Europe, but also in Asia and North America. Currently, it has more than 5,000 stores in 88 countries, and these stores can be found in some truly pricey locations: the Champs-Elysees in Paris, Fifth Avenue in New York, Galleria in Dallas, Ginza in Tokyo, Queen's Road Central in Hong Kong, and Huaihai Road in Shanghai.

UNDERSTANDING THE READING

A Check (✓) three statements that best summarize the writer's main ideas.

☐ 1. Safeguarding main breeding areas should be a top priority for tiger conservation.
☐ 2. It is a positive sign that tigers have been spotted outside of tiger reserves in India.
☐ 3. We should not accept the idea the tiger will continue to be a rare species; it might die out completely.
☐ 4. Patrolling and monitoring core tiger areas can help to increase tiger po...
☐ 5. The last few decades of tiger conservation strategies have generally be... successful.
☐ 6. Establishing land corridors for Indian tigers is probably unrealistic as a... strategy.

B Match each question with the correct answer. Three items are extra.

1. When did the world first realize that tigers were endangered? _____
2. How many tigers were estimated to be alive in the early 1980s? _____
3. What percentage of the world's tigers lives in India? _____
4. How many tigers are in Ranthambore? _____
5. Approximately how many tigers in India live outside of tiger reserves? _____
6. What year was the St. Petersburg Global Tiger Summit? _____
7. How many countries have natural tiger habitats? _____

C Complete the chart with information from the reading.

Problem: Tigers are endangered	
Possible Reasons	Possible Solutions
Past conservation efforts were not effective	
Growth of human populations	

DEVELOPING READING SKILLS

READING SKILL Understanding Sentences with Initial Phrases

Writers often put prepositional, time, and verbal phrases at the beginnings of sentences, before the main clause. Writers use initial phrases to vary their sentence structure and to change the emphasis in a sentence.
Founded in 1975, its parent company, Inditex, has become a leading global apparel retailer.
Since its initial public offering (IPO) in 2001, Inditex, ... has doubled the number of its stores.

A Look back at paragraphs C, D, E, and F in the reading passage. Find and underline all the initial phrases.

B Answer the questions. Use information from initial phrases you identified in A.

1. Why are customers motivated to visit Zara stores more frequently than other stores?
   a. because items in Zara stores are only available for a relatively short time
   b. because Zara will regularly offer huge discounts on many of its products
2. How has Zara developed a super responsive supply chain?
   a. by making most of its clothing in or near its headquarters
   b. by having factories in many different countries around the world
3. How do most fashion companies take advantage of economies of scale?
   a. by selling their items in huge stores
   b. by producing products in large batches
4. Why is Zara not worried about missing the boat when it comes to trends?
   a. because its designers are extremely good at predicting future fashion trends
   b. because it can keep up with trends by designing and making new products quickly

Boxes of ready-to-wear garments are prepared at Zara's headquarters in Arteixo, Spain.

RETHINKING BUSINESS 83

Video

PHOTO CONTEST

Brian Yen's winning photo from the 2014 National Geographic Photography Contest

BEFORE VIEWING

A How would you rate the photo above? Consider Griffiths's six criteria and discuss in a small group.

DISCUSSION

B Read the information. Then answer the questions.

LEARNING ABOUT THE TOPIC

Each year, National Geographic invites amateur photographers to enter their photographs into a competition. In 2014, people from more than 150 countries submitted photos representing three categories: people, places, and nature. Over 9,000 photos were submitted, but only a handful were chosen as winners. The winning entries all had one thing in common: they told a story. The grand prize winner, Brian Yen, received $10,000 and a trip to National Geographic headquarters. When asked why he takes pictures, he explained, "Photography to me is like going on an archaeological dig: It offers me a tool to interpret reality by dusting away the uninteresting bits to reveal the gem underneath. It's an exciting, creative, and exploratory process. "

1. What story does Yen's photo tell?

2. Why does Yen compare taking pictures to archaeology?

BEAUTY AND PERCEPTION **61**

◀ **NEW AND UPDATED** *Video* sections use National Geographic video clips to expand on the unit's reading passage and to give learners ideas and language for the unit's writing task.

◀ **NEW** An additional short reading passage provides integrated skills practice.

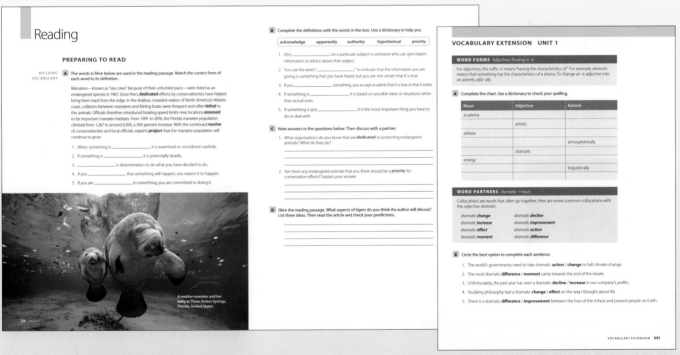

▲ **Key academic and thematic vocabulary** is practiced, and expanded throughout each unit.

▲ **NEW Vocabulary extension activities** cover word forms, word webs, collocations, affixes, and more, to boost learners' reading and writing fluency.

Writing Skills Practice

Pathways' approach to writing guides students through the writing process and develops learners' confidence in planning, drafting, revising, and editing.

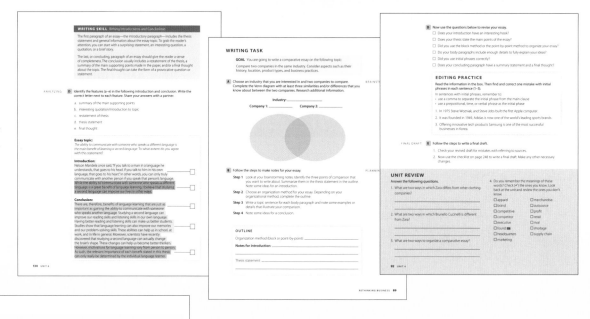

WRITING TASK

GOAL You are going to write a comparative essay on the following topic:

Compare two companies in the same industry. Consider aspects such as their history, location, product types, and business practices.

Writing Goals and ***Language for Writing*** ▶ sections provide the focus and scaffolding needed for learners to become successful writers.

▼ An **online workbook**, powered by MyELT, includes video clips and automatically graded activities for learners to practice the skills taught in the Student Books.

UPDATED Revising ▶ **Practice** sections incorporate realistic model essays and help learners refine their writing.

NEW Guided online writing ▶ **practice** provides reinforcement and consolidation of language skills, helping learners to become stronger and more confident writers.

CHANGING THE PLANET

1

A residential suburb in
Arizona, United States

THINK AND DISCUSS

1 In what ways have humans changed the planet?
2 What are some of the positive and negative effects
of the changes humans have made on the planet?

A Look at the maps and answer the questions.

1. What four types of human impact does the main map show?
2. Which regions experience the most deforestation, desertification, and pollution?
3. What are some causes of air pollution, deforestation, and desertification?

B Match the correct form of the words in blue to their definitions.

_____ (n) the layer of gases around a planet

_____ (n) a substance used by farmers to help crops grow

_____ (n) gradual destruction by natural causes such as the weather, the sea, and rivers

Deforestation

Loss of forest cover contributes to a buildup of carbon dioxide (a greenhouse gas) in the **atmosphere**. It also causes soil **erosion** and a loss of soil nutrients.

THE HUMAN IMPACT

Around the world, natural environments are under pressure from the release of air and water pollutants, and by the removal of vegetation to extract mineral resources or to create land for farming.

In more developed countries, industries create waste and pollution; farmers use **fertilizers** and pesticides that run off into water supplies; and motor vehicles release exhaust fumes into the air.

In less developed countries, forests are cut down for fuel or to clear land for farming; grasslands are turned into deserts as farmers and herders overuse the land; and expanding urban areas face problems of water quality and sanitation.

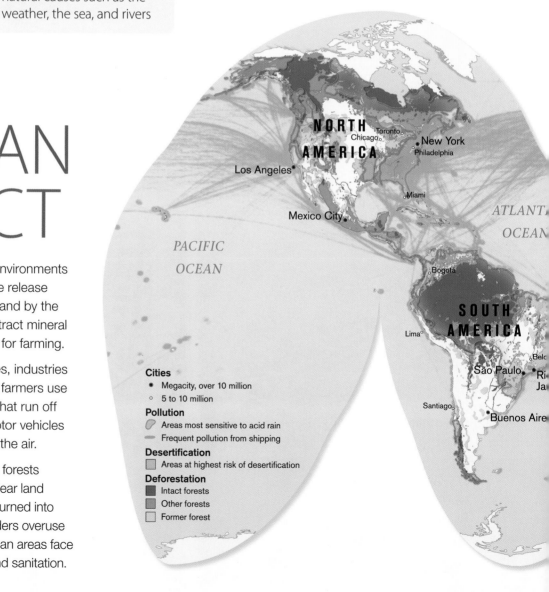

Cities
- • Megacity, over 10 million
- ○ 5 to 10 million

Pollution
- Areas most sensitive to acid rain
- Frequent pollution from shipping

Desertification
- Areas at highest risk of desertification

Deforestation
- Intact forests
- Other forests
- Former forest

Desertification

In semiarid and arid areas—which receive limited rainfall—land that is overgrazed or overcultivated can become desertlike.

Pollution

Poor air quality is a serious environmental problem in many parts of the world. Smoke from industrial plants may contain particles that contribute to acid rain.

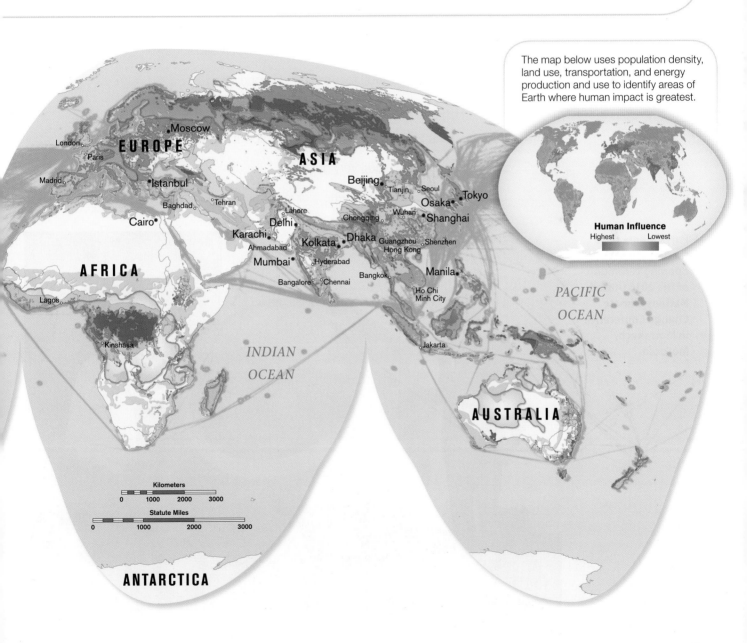

The map below uses population density, land use, transportation, and energy production and use to identify areas of Earth where human impact is greatest.

Human Influence
Highest   Lowest

London
Paris
Madrid
EUROPE
Moscow
Istanbul
Baghdad
Tehran
Cairo
ASIA
Beijing
Tianjin
Seoul
Osaka
Tokyo
Chongqing
Wuhan
Shanghai
Lahore
Delhi
Karachi
Ahmadabad
Kolkata
Dhaka
Guangzhou
Shenzhen
Hong Kong
Mumbai
Hyderabad
AFRICA
Bangalore
Chennai
Bangkok
Manila
Lagos
Ho Chi Minh City
Kinshasa
INDIAN OCEAN
Jakarta
PACIFIC OCEAN
AUSTRALIA

Kilometers
0   1000   2000   3000

Statute Miles
0   1000   2000   3000

ANTARCTICA

Reading

PREPARING TO READ

BUILDING
VOCABULARY

A The words in **blue** below are used in the reading passage. Match the correct form of each word to its definition.

Diplomats and scientists from around the world met to discuss climate issues at the 2016 United Nations Climate Change Conference in Marrakech, Morocco. The conference was **devoted to** discussing the reduction of global carbon emissions, which contribute to global warming. The dominant **perspective** on global warming is that it is a **consequence** of human activities. A **dramatic** increase in carbon emissions in the last several years has had a **profound** effect on the global climate. While most experts agree that it is impossible to completely **eliminate** carbon emissions, they do believe it is possible to cool down the planet.

1. _____ (adj) very noticeable; sudden and surprising

2. _____ (adj) focused only on one thing

3. _____ (v) to remove completely

4. _____ (n) a way of thinking about something

5. _____ (adj) very great

6. _____ (n) the effect or result of an action

▶ **Participants pose for a photo at the opening ceremony of the 2016 United Nations Climate Change Conference in Marrakech, Morocco.**

B Complete the sentences with the words in the box. Use a dictionary to help you.

| concept | criteria | current | essentially | satisfy | transform |

1. One of the _____ for naming a new animal species is that the name must be easy to remember.

2. A basic scientific _____ is cause and effect: the idea that an event is caused by or affected by another event.

3. Coal is _____ the remains of prehistoric plants. Over time, physical and chemical changes _____ ancient plant material into a substance that could be used as fuel.

4. Most animal species _____ the basic needs of their young until their offspring reach a certain age and can take care of themselves.

5. If our _____ efforts to lower carbon emissions are not significant enough to stop climate change, global warming may become worse in the future.

C Note answers to the questions below. Then discuss with a partner.

1. What are some of the **consequences** of human existence on the planet?

   _____

2. What do you think is the most **dramatic** consequence?

   _____

3. What are some **current** efforts to deal with these consequences?

   _____

D How do we know what Earth was like in the past? How do we know about plants or animals that existed in the past? Note your ideas below. Then discuss with a partner.

_____

_____

E Look at the photos and infographics in the reading and read the captions. Read the title and the first sentence of each paragraph. Circle your answers to the questions.

1. What do you think this reading is about? Circle your answer (a–c).

   It's an explanation of how _____ on the planet is changing the way people in the future might describe the current geological period.

   a. the effect of global warming
   b. the overall human impact
   c. the increasing population

2. What time period do you think *Anthropocene* describes?

   a. an ancient period   b. the current period   c. a future period

3. What area of science is this passage mainly about?

   a. biology   b. climatology   c. geology

THE HUMAN AGE

by Elizabeth Kolbert

Western Minnesota: Vast wheat fields and long train lines have created a distinctive human landscape in the Midwestern United States.

> Human beings have altered the planet so much in just the past century or two that we now have a new name for a new epoch: the Anthropocene.

1.1

The word *Anthropocene* was coined by Dutch chemist Paul Crutzen in 2002. Crutzen, who shared a Nobel Prize for discovering the effects of ozone-depleting compounds, was sitting at a scientific conference one day. The conference chairman kept referring to the Holocene, the epoch that began 11,500 years ago, at the end of the last ice age, and that—officially, at least—continues to this day.

"Let's stop it," Crutzen recalls blurting out. "We are no longer in the Holocene. We are in the Anthropocene." It was quiet in the room for a while. When the group took a coffee break, the Anthropocene was the main topic of conversation.

Way back in the 1870s, an Italian geologist named Antonio Stoppani proposed that people had introduced a new era, which he labeled the Anthropozoic. Stoppani's proposal was ignored; other scientists found it unscientific. The Anthropocene, by contrast, struck a chord. The human impact on the world has become a lot more obvious since Stoppani's day, in part because the size of the population has roughly quadrupled,[1] to nearly seven billion.

When Crutzen wrote up the Anthropocene idea in the journal *Nature*, the concept was immediately picked up by researchers working in a wide range of disciplines. Soon, it began to appear regularly in the scientific press. At first, most of the scientists using the new geologic term were not geologists. Jan Zalasiewicz, a British geologist, found the discussions intriguing. "I noticed that Crutzen's term was appearing in the serious literature, without quotation marks and without a sense of irony," he says.

In 2007, Zalasiewicz was serving as chairman of the Geological Society of London's Stratigraphy[2] Commission. At a meeting, he decided to ask his fellow stratigraphers what they thought of the Anthropocene. Twenty-one of twenty-two thought the concept had merit. The group agreed to look at it as a formal problem in geology. Would the Anthropocene satisfy the criteria used for naming a new epoch?

The rock record of the present doesn't exist yet, of course. So the question was: When it does, will human impacts show up as "stratigraphically significant"? The answer, Zalasiewicz's group decided, is yes—though not necessarily for the reasons you would expect.

[1] If something **quadruples**, it increases by a factor of four.
[2] **Stratigraphy** is a branch of geology concerned with the study of rock layers.

Earth's Geological Timeline

start of the Anthropocene?

Era	Period		Epoch	Millions of Years
Cenozoic	Quaternary		Holocene	
			Pleistocene	
	Neogene		Pliocene	1.5
			Miocene	
	Paleogene		Oligocene	2.3
			Eocene	
			Paleocene	
Mesozoic	Cretaceous			65
	Jurassic			
	Triassic			
Paleozoic	Permian			250
	Carboniferous	Pennsylvanian		
		Mississippian		
	Devonian			
	Silurian			
	Ordovician			
	Cambrian			
Precambrian	Proterozoic			540
	Archean			2500
	Hadean			3800
				4600

In geology, epochs are relatively short time spans, though they can extend for tens of millions of years. Periods, such as the Ordovician and the Cretaceous, last much longer, and eras, like the Mesozoic, longer still. The boundaries between epochs are defined by changes preserved in sedimentary rocks[3] —for example, the emergence of one type of commonly fossilized organism, or the disappearance of another.

G

PROBABLY THE MOST OBVIOUS way humans are altering the planet is by building cities, which are essentially vast stretches of man-made materials—steel, glass, concrete, and brick. But it turns out most cities are not good candidates for long-term preservation: they're built on land, and on land the forces of erosion tend to win out over those of sedimentation. From a geologic perspective, the most plainly visible human effects on the landscape today "may in some ways be the most transient,[4]" Zalasiewicz observes.

H

Humans have also transformed the world through farming; something like 38 percent of the planet's ice-free land is now devoted to agriculture. Here again, some of the effects that seem most significant today—runoff from the use of fertilizers on fields, for example—will leave behind only subtle traces at best. Future geologists are most likely to grasp the scale of 21st-century industrial agriculture from the pollen[5] record— from the monochrome[6] stretches of corn, wheat, and soy pollen that will have replaced the varied record left behind by rain forests or prairies.

[3] **Sedimentary rocks** are formed from sediment—solid material that settles at the bottom of a liquid.
[4] **Transient** describes a situation that lasts only a short time or is constantly changing.
[5] **Pollen** is a powder produced by flowers that fertilizes other flowers of the same species.
[6] If something is **monochrome**, it is all one color.

The leveling of the world's forests will send at least two coded signals to future stratigraphers, though deciphering the first may be tricky. Massive soil erosion is causing increasing sedimentation[7] in some parts of the world—but at the same time, the dams we've built on most of the world's major rivers are holding back sediment that would otherwise be washed to sea. The second signal of deforestation should come through clearer. Loss of forest habitat is a major cause of extinctions, which are now happening at a rate hundreds or even thousands of times higher than during most of the past half billion years. If current trends continue, the rate may soon be tens of thousands of times higher.

Probably the most significant change, from a geologic perspective, is one that's invisible to us—the change in the composition of the atmosphere. Carbon dioxide emissions are colorless, odorless, and—in an immediate sense—harmless. But their warming effects could easily push global temperatures to levels that have not been seen for millions of years. Some plants and animals are already shifting their ranges toward the Poles, and those shifts will leave traces in the fossil record. Some species will not survive the warming at all. Meanwhile, rising temperatures could eventually raise sea levels 20 feet or more.

Long after our cars, cities, and factories have turned to dust, the consequences of burning billions of tons' worth of coal and oil are likely to be clearly discernible. As carbon dioxide warms the planet, it also seeps into the oceans and acidifies them. Sometime this century, they may become acidified to the point that corals can no longer construct reefs, which would register in the geologic record as a "reef gap." Reef gaps have marked each of the past five major mass extinctions. The most recent one—which is believed to have been caused by the impact of an asteroid—took place 65 million years ago, at the end of the Cretaceous period; it eliminated not just the dinosaurs but also the plesiosaurs, pterosaurs, and ammonites.[8] Since then, there has been nothing to match the scale of the changes that we are now seeing in our oceans. To future geologists, Zalasiewicz says, our impact may look as sudden and profound as that of an asteroid.

---

[7] Sedimentation is the process by which solid material—especially earth and pieces of rock—settles at the bottom of a liquid.
[8] Plesiosaurs, pterosaurs, and ammonites are extinct prehistoric organisms.

Colorado River Delta, Mexico:
Aerial photography can illustrate the human impact on Earth's landscape.

> **"** Do we decide the Anthropocene's here, or do we wait 20 years and things will be even worse? **"**

IF WE HAVE INDEED entered a new epoch, then when exactly did it begin? When did human impacts rise to the level of geologic significance?

William Ruddiman, a paleoclimatologist at the University of Virginia, has proposed that the invention of agriculture some 8,000 years ago—and the deforestation that resulted—led to an increase in atmospheric CO_2 just large enough to stave off what otherwise would have been the start of a new ice age. In his view, humans have

Trotternish, Isle of Skye: Millions of years of history are recorded in the rocks of Scotland. Are we creating a new chapter in Earth's geological history?

been the dominant force on the planet practically since the start of the Holocene. Crutzen has suggested that the Anthropocene began in the late 18th century, when, ice cores show, carbon dioxide levels began what has since proved to be an uninterrupted rise. Other scientists put the beginning of the new epoch in the middle of the 20th century, when the rates of both population growth and consumption accelerated rapidly.

Zalasiewicz now heads a working group of the International Commission on Stratigraphy (ICS) that is tasked with officially determining whether the Anthropocene deserves to be incorporated into the geologic timescale. A final decision will require votes by both the ICS and its parent organization, the International Union of Geological Sciences. The process is likely to take years. As it drags on, the decision may well become easier. Some scientists argue that we've not yet reached the start of the Anthropocene—not because we haven't had a **dramatic** impact on the planet, but because the next several decades are likely to prove even more stratigraphically significant than the past few centuries. "Do we decide the Anthropocene's here, or do we wait 20 years and things will be even worse?" says Mark Williams, a geologist and colleague of Zalasiewicz's at the University of Leicester in England.

Crutzen, who started the debate, thinks its real value won't lie in revisions to geology textbooks. His purpose is broader: He wants to focus our attention on the consequences of our collective action—and on how we might still avert the worst. "What I hope," he says, "is that the term *Anthropocene* will be a warning to the world."

Adapted from "The Age of Man," by Elizabeth Kolbert: National Geographic Magazine, March 2011

National Magazine Award winner Elizabeth Kolbert has written extensively about environmental issues for *National Geographic Magazine, The New Yorker,* and other publications. Her book *The Sixth Extinction* won the 2015 Pulitzer Prize for general nonfiction.

UNDERSTANDING THE READING

UNDERSTANDING
MAIN IDEAS

A Note answers to the questions below.

1. What is the purpose of Kolbert's article? Complete the main idea.

   Kolbert's purpose is to present the idea of a new _____ and to show how our human impact will be noted in the future.

2. What does "Anthropocene" mean? Explain it in your own words.

   _____

   _____

3. What four main areas does Kolbert examine for signs of human impact?

   cities, _____

UNDERSTANDING
MAIN IDEAS

B The reading passage has three main parts. Where could you place each of these section heads? Write paragraph letters: **A**, **G**, and **L**.

Section Head	Before Paragraph ...
How We Are Changing the Planet	_____
Tracing the Origins of the Anthropocene	_____
A New Perspective on Earth's History	_____

UNDERSTANDING
DETAILS

C Note answers to the questions below. Then discuss with a partner.

1. When was the idea of a new era first proposed? What was it called? Why did people not take it seriously?

   _____

   _____

   _____

2. Why did Crutzen's ideas gain more support than Stoppani's?

   _____

   _____

   _____

3. What are two effects of cutting down forests?

   _____

   _____

   _____

4. How does climate change affect plants and animals? How is it affecting the oceans?

   _____

   _____

   _____

   _____

D Complete the chart summarizing the human impact on our planet. Then discuss this question in a small group: Of the four kinds of human impact, which do you think will leave the most obvious record in the future? Why?

	The Human Impact	Will It Leave a Trace? Why, or Why Not?
Cities	building structures made of 1_____	No—structures built on land; 2_____ may make them disappear
Farming	farming 3_____ percent of the available land	4_____—but only from the 5_____ record of the shift from a variety of plants to a few types
Forests	6_____ trees	Maybe—sedimentation and 7_____ may be noticed
Atmosphere	8_____ the atmosphere	Most likely—shifts in habitat range will leave traces in 9_____; the world's 10_____ will become acidified and coral will no longer be able to construct reefs

E Look at the timeline on page 8 and note answers to the questions below. Then discuss your ideas with a partner.

1. What era, period, and epoch are we currently living in?

   Era: _____   Period: _____

   Epoch: _____ or _____

2. When did the current era begin?

   _____

3. How do scientists decide when one epoch ends and another one begins?

   _____

   _____

The acidification of the ocean, caused by high levels of carbon dioxide in the atmosphere, could cause coral reefs to die out.

> **CRITICAL THINKING** In a reading passage that presents an argument, the writer argues for one side of an issue and provides evidence to support their position. When you read a passage that presents an argument, first identify the writer's position. Then **analyze** the writer's evidence. Is it from a reliable source? Is it detailed? Is it current?

CRITICAL THINKING: ANALYZING EVIDENCE

F In the reading passage, what evidence does the writer present in support of either side of the main argument? Take notes in the chart. Then discuss answers to the questions below with a partner.

Argument: Humans are having such a great impact on the planet that the Holocene epoch is over, and we are now living in a new epoch: the Anthropocene.	
Evidence For	**Evidence Against**

1. Is the evidence on both sides balanced, or is there more evidence for one side than the other?
2. Do the facts and opinions come from reliable sources? Is the information relevant and up to date?

CRITICAL THINKING: GUESSING MEANING FROM CONTEXT

G Find and underline the following words and expressions in the reading passage. Use context to guess their meanings. Then match the sentence parts.

1. Para A: If a word is **coined by** someone, ＿＿   a. it continues for a long time.

2. Para C: If an idea **struck a chord**, ＿＿   b. you can detect it.

3. Para I: If you **decipher** something, ＿＿   c. you figure out the meaning of it.

4. Para K: If a consequence is **discernible**, ＿＿   d. you prevent it from happening.

5. Para M: If you **stave off** an event, ＿＿   e. it was invented by that person.

6. Para N: When something **drags on**, ＿＿   f. other people thought it sounded logical.

DEVELOPING READING SKILLS

READING SKILL Understanding Cohesion

Cohesion refers to the way that ideas are linked in a text. Writers use certain techniques (sometimes called "cohesive devices") to refer to ideas mentioned elsewhere in the passage. Some of these techniques include pronouns (*one*[s], *another*, *the other*), demonstratives (*this*, *that*, *these*, *those*), and synonyms.

Look at these examples from "The Human Age."

> In 2002, when Crutzen wrote up <u>the Anthropocene idea</u> in the journal Nature, <u>the concept</u> was immediately picked up by researchers working in a wide range of disciplines.

The writer uses a synonym, *the concept*, to refer to *the idea* in the first part of the sentence.

> Wilson calculates that human <u>biomass</u> is already a hundred times larger than <u>that</u> of any other large animal species that has ever walked the Earth.

In this example, the writer uses *that* to refer to *biomass*.

Note: The referent—the word or idea that is referred to—is not always close to the cohesive device. It may be in a different part of the sentence, or in a different sentence or section of the text.

A Circle the word or idea that each underlined word in these extracts refers to.

ANALYZING

1. Paragraph D: When Crutzen wrote up the Anthropocene idea in the journal *Nature*, the concept was immediately picked up by researchers working in a wide range of disciplines. Soon, <u>it</u> began to appear regularly in the scientific press.

    a. the researchers   b. the journal   c. the concept

2. Paragraph G: But it turns out most cities are not good candidates for long-term preservation for the simple reason that they're built on land, and on land the forces of erosion tend to win out over <u>those</u> of sedimentation.

    a. forces   b. cities   c. candidates

B Find the following excerpts in "The Human Age." Write the words or ideas that each underlined word or phrase refers to.

ANALYZING

1. Paragraph D: At first, most of the scientists using <u>the new geologic term</u> were not geologists. _____

2. Sidebar: The boundaries between epochs are defined by changes preserved in sedimentary rocks—for example, the emergence of one type of commonly fossilized organism, or the disappearance of <u>another</u>. _____

3. Paragraph J: Probably the most significant change, from a geologic perspective, is <u>one</u> that's invisible to us—the change in the composition of the atmosphere. _____

4. Paragraph K: The most recent <u>one</u>—which is believed to have been caused by the impact of an asteroid—took place 65 million years ago, at the end of the Cretaceous period. _____

Video

TREES OF LIFE

Deforestation threatens the habitats of many species of animals.

BEFORE VIEWING

DISCUSSION

A How does deforestation affect our planet? Note your ideas below. Then discuss with a partner.

_____

_____

LEARNING ABOUT THE TOPIC

B Read the information. Then answer the questions.

Rain forests provide habitats for thousands of species of animals. However, they also provide humans with many useful resources such as fruits and spices. Perhaps the most valuable rain forest resources, however, are medicinal plants. Scientists use rain forest plants to create drugs for many serious health problems. The bark of the cinchona tree, for example, is used to make quinine—a medication used to treat malaria. It is thought that scientists have analyzed less than one percent of rain forest plants, so there are probably hundreds, if not thousands, of medicinal plants that remain undiscovered.

1. What benefits of rain forests are mentioned in the paragraph above?

_____

2. How do you think deforestation would affect our ability to treat serious illnesses?

_____

C Read these extracts from the video. Match the correct form of each **bold** word to its definition.

> "At the current rate of **destruction**, the world's rain forests will completely disappear within a hundred years."
>
> "Forests are also destroyed as a result of growing urban sprawl, as land is developed for **dwellings**."
>
> "And while some plant and animal species are gone forever, **combatting** deforestation can help prevent further loss of biodiversity."

1. _____ (v) to fight against

2. _____ (n) a house or home

3. _____ (n) the act of damaging something completely

WHILE VIEWING

A ▶ Read the sentences below. Watch the video. Circle **T** for true or **F** for false.

a. Transportation produces more greenhouse gases than forestry and agriculture. **T F**

b. Over 80 percent of land animals live in forests. **T F**

c. Increases in the size of urban areas is the primary cause of deforestation. **T F**

B ▶ Watch the video again. Complete the notes below.

DEFORESTATION	
Effects	**Causes**
1. Increases greenhouse gases in two ways: • ¹_____ releases CO_2 • Forests help to ²_____ 2. Destroys ³_____ Also effects people who use forests for ⁴_____	1. ⁵_____ is the main cause. 2. Logging for ⁶_____ industries 3. Increasing ⁷_____

AFTER VIEWING

A What are two signs of deforestation that future stratigraphers will notice? Look again at the reading passage for ideas. Note your answer below. Then discuss with a partner.

_____

_____

Writing

EXPLORING WRITTEN ENGLISH

A The following words and phrases can be useful when writing about the human impact on the planet. Find them in the reading passage. Use the context to guess their meanings. Then complete each definition.

> **preservation** (paragraph G) **relatively** (sidebar) **subtle** (paragraph H)
>
> **tasked with** (paragraph N) **determine** (paragraph N) **avert** (paragraph O)

1. To _____ something is to prevent it from happening.

2. If you _____ something, you figure it out.

3. If a person or group is _____ a duty, it is their responsibility to do it.

4. _____ refers to the protection of something over time.

5. If something is _____ big, it is big in comparison to something else.

6. If something is _____, it is not very noticeable.

B Read the sentences. Circle the words that the underlined words refer to.

1. Crutzen, who started the debate, thinks <u>its</u> real value won't lie in revisions to geology textbooks.
2. The process is likely to take years. As <u>it</u> drags on, the decision may well become easier.
3. Crutzen has suggested that the Anthropocene began in the late 18th century … Other scientists put the beginning of <u>the new epoch</u> in the middle of the 20th century …
4. As carbon dioxide warms the planet, <u>it</u> also seeps into the oceans and acidifies <u>them</u>.
5. To future geologists, Zalasiewicz says, our impact may look as sudden and profound as <u>that</u> of an asteroid.

Flower fields in California, United States

Writers use cohesive devices to emphasize key concepts they have already mentioned and to avoid repetition. Cohesive devices include reference words such as *it*, *these*, *those*, and *that*. They also include synonyms and word forms.

Reference Words and Synonyms:

In 2002, when Crutzen wrote up the Anthropocene idea in the journal *Nature*, **the concept** was immediately picked up by researchers working in a wide range of disciplines. Soon it began to appear regularly in the scientific press.

The writer uses *the concept* and *it* to refer to *the Anthropocene idea*.

Word Forms:

Way back in the 1870s, an Italian geologist named Antonio Stoppani proposed that people had introduced a new era, which he labeled the Anthropozoic. Stoppani's **proposal** was ignored; other scientists found it unscientific.

The writer uses *proposal* to refer to what Stoppani *proposed*.

C Use the cues to complete the second sentence in each pair below. Use reference words, synonyms, or word forms for the underlined words in the first sentence.

USING COHESIVE DEVICES

1. Cities are filled with structures made of glass, steel, and concrete. Many people might think that _____ are indestructible materials. (reference word)

2. Farming has had a huge impact on the world's landscapes. Around 38 percent of our planet's ice-free land is now used solely for _____. (synonym)

3. Humans have destroyed forests, built over animal habitats, and heated up the atmosphere with CO_2 emissions. Of all these _____, the changes in the atmosphere may leave the most lasting traces. (synonym)

4. By creating pedestrian-only streets in city centers, planners are reducing the amount of time people spend in cars. This _____ in car use will have a positive impact on the environment. (word form)

5. Chemicals used in pesticides may harm people and animals. These _____ compounds can have a negative impact on the soil and water as well. (word form)

WRITING SKILL Reviewing Essay Writing

An essay is a short piece of writing that includes an **introduction**, a **body**, and a **conclusion**. The introduction presents general information on the topic, and usually includes a **thesis statement**. The thesis statement presents the main idea of the entire essay. The body paragraphs support the thesis with facts, details, explanations, and other information. **Transitions** between paragraphs help the reader follow the essay. The conclusion restates the thesis and leaves the reader with a final thought on the topic.

You usually write an essay in response to an **essay prompt**. The prompt might be an instruction (*Describe/Explain . . .*), or it might be a question (*Why . . . ? To what extent . . . ? How . . . ?*). When you respond to a prompt, think about your position on the topic (which will become your thesis statement) and ways to support or explain your position (which may become the topic sentences of your body paragraphs).

CRITICAL THINKING: EVALUATING

D Read the following essay prompt. Circle the best thesis statement for it. Why is it the best? Discuss your answer with a partner.

What are some ways that people can help heal the planet through their food choices?

a. People can make much better food choices.

b. People can help heal the planet by making environmentally friendly food choices.

c. It's important that we start caring about the future of the planet right now.

CRITICAL THINKING: EVALUATING

E Think about ways to support or explain the thesis statement. Assume you are going to write three body paragraphs. Check (✓) the three best supporting ideas from the list below.

Make food choices that _____.

☐ a. are cheap

☐ b. promote health

☐ c. don't contribute to pollution

☐ d. preserve endangered species

☐ e. use fewer resources such as water

APPLYING

F Complete topic sentences for three body paragraphs based on the ideas you chose in exercise **E**.

One way that our food choices can help heal the planet is _____

_____

Another way is _____

_____

Finally, _____

_____

DISCUSSION

G Discuss the following essay prompt. Think of a good thesis statement and at least three possible ideas to support it. Share your ideas with a partner.

Describe new policies that would improve the quality of life at your college or school.

WRITING TASK

> **GOAL** You are going to write an essay on the following topic:
>
> Describe how the activities of a charity or a nonprofit organization are having a positive impact on the planet.

A Choose a charity or a nonprofit organization that you want to write about. Then think about how its activities are having a positive impact on the planet. Write as many activities and impacts in the chart as you can. Share your ideas with a partner.

BRAINSTORMING

Organization: _____

Activities	Impacts (Effects)
e.g., cleans plastic out of the ocean	e.g., protects marine life habitats

B Follow the steps to make notes for your essay.

PLANNING

Step 1 Write a thesis statement in the outline below.

Step 2 Write a topic sentence about each of the organization's activities for each body paragraph. Then write two or three examples, details, or facts that explain how each activity affects the planet.

Step 3 Note some ideas for an introduction and a conclusion for your essay.

OUTLINE

Thesis statement: _____
_____

Notes for Introduction: _____

Body Paragraph 1: Topic sentence: _____
_____

Details: _____
_____

Body Paragraph 2: Topic sentence: _____
_____

Details: _____
_____

Body Paragraph 3: Topic sentence: _____
_____

Details: _____
_____

Notes for Conclusion: _____
_____

REVISING PRACTICE

The draft below is a model of the essay you are writing. Follow the steps to create a better second draft.

1. Add the sentences (a–c) in the most suitable spaces.

   a. This reduces energy use as well as cost.
   b. By instituting these and other methods to make cities more livable and environmentally friendly, we can look forward to a happy and healthy future as our cities grow.
   c. Green spaces have a positive impact on a community.

2. Now fix the following problems (a–c) with the essay.

   a. Replace the **bold** word in paragraph B with a cohesive device.
   b. Replace the **bold** word in paragraph C with a cohesive device.
   c. Cross out one sentence that does not relate to the topic of the essay in paragraph D.

A

Cities are growing in size and in population. Will they have a harmful impact on the environment as they grow? Not necessarily. Many city planners have solutions to make cities and the people who live in them healthier and happier, while at the same time having a positive impact on the environment. Three ways to improve cities include creating green spaces, developing mixed-use areas, and encouraging building owners to transform their rooftops into gardens.

B

_____ **Green spaces** are protected areas that remain undeveloped, such as parks or other open areas. Increasing the number of them in a city has several advantages. Green spaces make a city more attractive, as plants and other features—such as streams and rocks—are left in their natural state. They also provide peaceful recreation areas for city dwellers. People can walk, hike, bicycle, and picnic in these areas away from the hustle and bustle of city life. Trees also shelter the area from the noise and traffic of the city while improving the air quality.

C

Another way to improve the quality of life in cities is the development of mixed-use areas. **Mixed-use** areas combine several purposes in one space. One of these areas, for example, may contain offices and businesses, apartments, and entertainment facilities. Ideally, mixed-use developments attract people who want to live and work in the same area. The benefits to the community are significant because these developments allow people to reduce the amount of time they spend in cars— driving to work and running errands—which in turn reduces air pollution. Creating mixed-use areas with pedestrian- and bicycle-only streets further lessens the impact on the environment, and it can also encourage better health and fitness as citizens spend less time in cars.

D

Finally, encouraging building owners to convert their rooftops into high-rise gardens and farms can bring about dramatic changes to city life and improve the environment at the same time. Rooftop gardens insulate buildings. For example, in areas that have hot summer weather, rooftop gardens can cool buildings so that they don't require as much air conditioning. _____ Gardens that are used to grow organic fruits and vegetables—as opposed to those grown with chemical compounds—can also improve the quality of life for city dwellers, especially if they live in areas where access to fresh produce is limited. Organic fruits and vegetables are increasingly available in many cities. Limiting the use of harmful pesticides through organic gardening is good for the planet and for human health, too.

E

Green spaces, mixed-use areas, and rooftop gardens are just a few of the ways that we can lessen the impact of cities on the planet. _____

D Now use the questions below to revise your essay.

REVISED DRAFT

☐ Does your introduction provide relevant background information on the topic?

☐ Does your thesis state the main points of the essay?

☐ Do your body paragraphs include enough details to fully explain your ideas?

☐ Did you use cohesive devices to avoid repetition?

☐ Do all your sentences relate to the main idea?

☐ Does your concluding paragraph have a summary statement and a final thought?

▼ **A chef picks bay leaves from the roof garden of a hotel in Vancouver, Canada.**

EDITING PRACTICE

Read the information below. Then edit the sentences (1–3) to make them clearer.

When using cohesive devices, remember to:

• use pronouns that match the referent in gender and number.

• make sure a pronoun clearly refers to a specific word or idea. Sometimes it's better to repeat words or use synonyms for clarity.

• choose the correct synonym when using a dictionary or thesaurus.

1. One reason to limit the use of pesticides is that it contains harmful compounds.

2. Some people are installing rooftop gardens and using solar panels in their homes. It can save money and resources.

3. Many fish species have become extinct and, as a result, there is less biodiversity in our oceans. They are a problem, because they upset the natural balance of the oceans' ecosystems.

FINAL DRAFT **E** **Follow these steps to write a final draft.**

1. Check your revised draft for mistakes with cohesive devices.

2. Now use the checklist on page 248 to write a final draft. Make any other necessary changes.

UNIT REVIEW

Answer the following questions.

1. What are three examples of the human impact on our planet?

_____

_____

2. Why are forests important to our planet?

_____

_____

3. What is an example of a cohesive device?

_____

_____

4. Do you remember the meanings of these words? Check (✓) the ones you know. Look back at the unit and review the ones you don't know.

☐ atmosphere   ☐ erosion AWL

☐ concept AWL   ☐ essentially

☐ consequence AWL   ☐ fertilizer

☐ criteria AWL   ☐ perspective AWL

☐ current   ☐ profound

☐ devoted to AWL   ☐ satisfy

☐ dramatic AWL   ☐ transform AWL

☐ eliminate AWL

ON THE EDGE

2

A two-week-old rescued orphan elephant with her keeper in Nairobi National Park, Kenya

THINK AND DISCUSS

1 What endangered species are you aware of?
2 What are some reasons these animals are endangered?

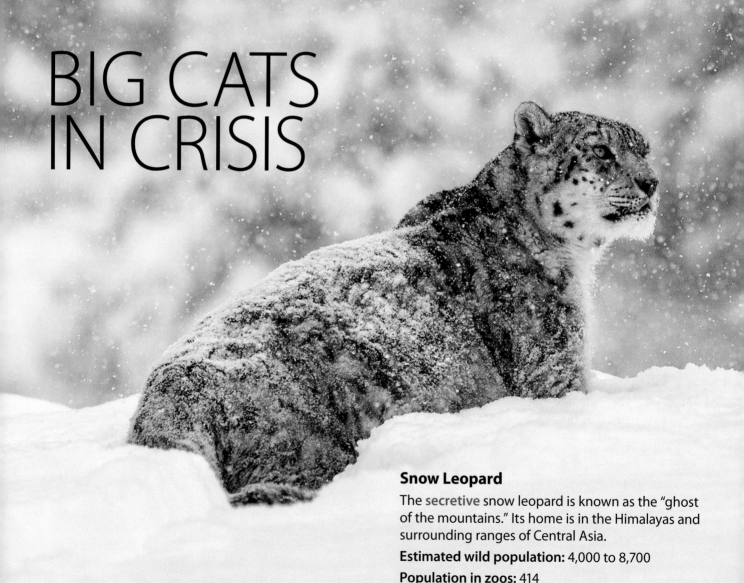

A **Look at the information on these pages and answer the questions.**

1. Which big cat on these pages do you think is most in danger? Why?

2. Why do you think conservationists think it is important to protect these animals?

B **Match the words in blue to their definitions.**

_____ (n) animals that kill and eat other animals

_____ (n) the animals that another animal eats for food

_____ (n) the illegal catching and/or killing of animals

_____ (adj) possible and practical to do or achieve

_____ (adj) hiding your feelings or actions from others

BIG CATS IN CRISIS

Snow Leopard

The secretive snow leopard is known as the "ghost of the mountains." Its home is in the Himalayas and surrounding ranges of Central Asia.

Estimated wild population: 4,000 to 8,700

Population in zoos: 414

Status: Vulnerable

The big cats on these pages are all in danger of disappearing from the wild. A major reason is loss of habitat resulting from human population growth in the areas where they live. Additional threats are posed by illegal **poaching** for skins and other body parts, and killing by ranchers when the cats eat their livestock. Conservationists, however, believe it is still **feasible** to save these **predators**.

Lion

Lions once roamed across Africa and into Asia; today, the largest lion population is in Tanzania.

Estimated wild population: 20,000 to 30,000

Population in zoos: 1,888

Status: Vulnerable

Cheetah

The cheetah uses its incredible speed to chase down its **prey**. It is found mainly in east and southwest Africa; another 70–110 live in Iran.

Estimated wild population: 7,000 to 10,000

Population in zoos: 1,015

Status: Vulnerable

Tiger

The biggest cat, with some males weighing over 600 pounds (270 kilograms). Three tiger subspecies have gone extinct since the 1930s; four or five other subspecies survive in Asia.

Estimated wild population: Fewer than 4,000

Population in zoos: 1,660

Status: Endangered

Reading

PREPARING TO READ

BUILDING
VOCABULARY

A The words in blue below are used in the reading passage. Match the correct form of each word to its definition.

Manatees—known as "sea cows" because of their unhurried pace—were listed as an endangered species in 1967. Since then, **dedicated** efforts by conservationists have helped bring them back from the edge. In the shallow, crowded waters of North America's Atlantic coast, collisions between manatees and fishing boats were frequent and often **lethal** to the animals. Officials therefore introduced boating speed limits near locations **assessed** to be important manatee habitats. From 1991 to 2016, the Florida manatee population climbed from 1,267 to around 6,300, a 500 percent increase. With the continued **resolve** of conservationists and local officials, experts **project** that the manatee population will continue to grow.

1. When something is _____, it is examined or considered carefully.

2. If something is _____, it is potentially deadly.

3. _____ is determination to do what you have decided to do.

4. If you _____ that something will happen, you expect it to happen.

5. If you are _____ to something, you are committed to doing it.

A mother manatee and her baby at Three Sisters Springs, Florida, United States

B Complete the definitions with the words in the box. Use a dictionary to help you.

| acknowledge | apparently | authority | hypothetical | priority |

1. A(n) _____ on a particular subject is someone who can give expert information or advice about that subject.

2. You use the word "_____" to indicate that the information you are giving is something that you have heard, but you are not certain that it is true.

3. If you _____ something, you accept or admit that it is true or that it exists.

4. If something is _____, it is based on possible ideas or situations rather than actual ones.

5. If something is a(n) _____, it is the most important thing you have to do or deal with.

C Note answers to the questions below. Then discuss with a partner.

1. What organizations do you know that are **dedicated** to protecting endangered animals? What do they do?

_____
_____
_____

2. Are there any endangered animals that you think should be a **priority** for conservation efforts? Explain your answer.

_____
_____
_____

D Skim the reading passage. What aspects of tigers do you think the author will discuss? List three ideas. Then read the article and check your predictions.

_____
_____
_____
_____

A CRY FOR THE TIGER

by Caroline Alexander

A lone tiger hunts in the forests of northern Sumatra, Indonesia.

> We have the means to save the mightiest cat
>
> on Earth. But do we have the will?

🔊 1.2

Dawn, and mist covers the forest. Only a short stretch of red dirt track can be seen. Suddenly—emerging from the red-gold haze of dust and misted light—a tigress walks into view. First, she stops to rub her right-side whiskers against a roadside tree. Then she crosses the road and rubs her left-side whiskers. Then she turns to regard us with a look of bored indifference.

Consider the tiger, how she is formed. The claws of a tiger are up to four inches long and retractable,[1] like those of a domestic cat; her teeth can shatter bone. While able to achieve bursts above 35 miles an hour, the tiger is a predator built for strength, not sustained speed. Short, powerful legs propel her lethal attacks. The eye of the tiger is backlit by a membrane, a thin piece of skin that reflects light through the retina—the secret of the animal's famous night vision and glowing night eyes. The roar of the tiger—*Aaaaauuuunnnn!*—can carry more than a mile.

For weeks, I had been traveling through some of the best tiger habitats in Asia, but never before had I seen a tiger. Partly this was because of the animal's legendarily secretive nature. The tiger is powerful enough to kill and drag prey five times its weight, yet it can move through high grass, forest, and even water in unnerving silence. Those who have witnessed—or survived—an attack commonly report that the tiger "came from nowhere."

But the other reason for the lack of sightings is that the ideal tiger landscapes have very few tigers. The tiger has been a threatened species for most of my lifetime, and its rareness has come to be regarded—like its dramatic coloring—as a defining attribute. The common view that the tiger will continue to be "rare" or "threatened" is no longer tenable.[3] In the early 21st century, tigers in the wild face complete annihilation. "This is about making decisions as if we're in an emergency room," says Tom Kaplan, co-founder of Panthera, an organization dedicated to big cats. "This is it."

The tiger's enemies are well-known. Loss of habitat is exacerbated by exploding human populations. Poverty contributes to the poaching of prey animals. Above all, there is the dark threat of a black market for tiger parts. Less acknowledged are decades of botched conservation strategies. The tiger population, dispersed among Asia's 13 tiger countries, is estimated at fewer than 4,000 animals, though many conservationists believe there are hundreds less than that. To put this number in perspective: Global alarm for the species was first sounded in 1969, and early in the 1980s it was estimated that some 8,000 tigers remained in the wild. So decades of concern for tigers—not to mention millions of dollars donated by well-meaning individuals—has failed to prevent the loss of perhaps half of an already threatened population.

[1]If something is **retractable,** it can be moved in and out or back and forth.
[2]The **retina** is the area at the back of the eye.

[3]If an argument is **tenable,** it is reasonable and can be successfully defended against criticism.

> " If the core breeding grounds are lost, you will have tiger landscapes with no tigers. "

My determination to see a wild tiger in my lifetime brought me to Ranthambore Tiger Reserve, one of 40 in India. India is home to some 50 percent of the world's wild tigers. The 2010 census reported a maximum estimate of 1,909 in the country—up 20 percent from the previous estimate. While this is welcome news, most authorities regard the new figure as reflecting better census methods rather than growth of the tiger population: Tiger counts, in India or elsewhere, are still at best only estimates. A modest 41 of these tigers were living in Ranthambore.

Reserves such as Ranthambore exist as islands of fragile habitat in a vast sea of humanity, yet tigers can range over a hundred miles, seeking prey, mates, and territory. An unwelcome revelation of the new census is that nearly a third of India's tigers live outside tiger reserves, a situation that is dangerous for both humans and animals. Prey and tigers can only disperse if there are recognized corridors[4] of land between protected areas to allow safe passage. No less critical, such passages would serve as genetic corridors, essential to the long-term survival of the species.

It is a heady[5] experience to see an idealistic map of Asia's tiger landscapes linked by these not-yet-existent corridors. A spiderweb of green lines weaves among core tiger populations, forming a network that includes breathtaking extremes of habitat—Himalayan foothills, jungle, swamp, forest, grasslands. However, close examination breaks the spell. The places that have actual tigers—here-and-now,

[4]**Corridors** are strips of land that connect one place to another.
[5]A **heady** experience strongly affects your senses, such as, by making you feel excited.

Tiger cubs at a water hole in Bandhavgarh National Park, India

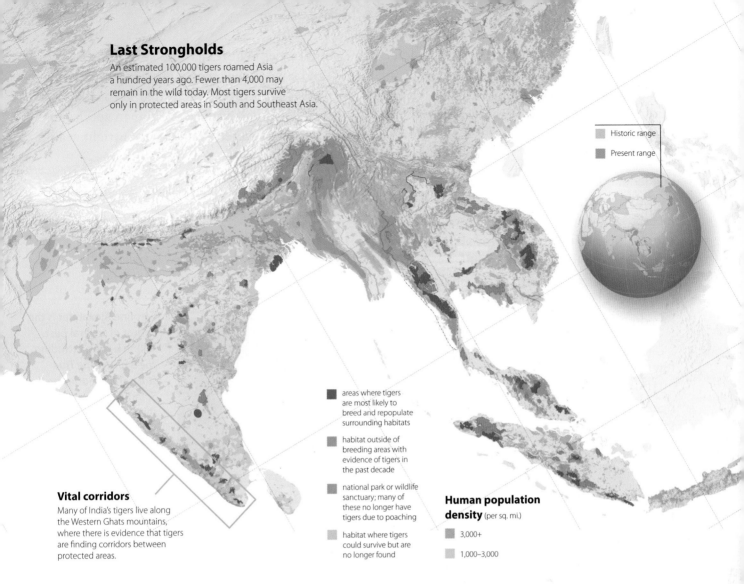

Last Strongholds

An estimated 100,000 tigers roamed Asia a hundred years ago. Fewer than 4,000 may remain in the wild today. Most tigers survive only in protected areas in South and Southeast Asia.

Historic range

Present range

areas where tigers are most likely to breed and repopulate surrounding habitats

habitat outside of breeding areas with evidence of tigers in the past decade

national park or wildlife sanctuary; many of these no longer have tigers due to poaching

habitat where tigers could survive but are no longer found

Human population density (per sq. mi.)

3,000+

1,000–3,000

Vital corridors

Many of India's tigers live along the Western Ghats mountains, where there is evidence that tigers are finding corridors between protected areas.

flesh-and-blood tigers—as opposed to hypothetical ones, are represented by a scattering of brown-colored spots. The master plan is ambitious, but is it feasible? Over the next decade, infrastructure projects—the kind of development that often destroys habitat—are projected to average some $750 billion a year in Asia.

"I've never met a head of state who says, 'Look, we're a poor country, if it comes between tigers and people, you just have to write off tigers,'" said Alan Rabinowitz, an authority on tigers and the CEO of Panthera. "The governments don't want to lose their most majestic animal. They consider it part of what makes their country what it is, part of the cultural heritage. They won't sacrifice a lot to save it, but if they can see a way to save it, they will usually do it."

Seeing a way has proved difficult due to the variety of tiger strategies, programs, and initiatives competing for attention—and funding. Long-term conservation must focus on all aspects of a tiger landscape: core breeding populations, sanctuaries, wildlife corridors, and the surrounding human communities. In an ideal world, all would be funded; as it is, different agencies adopt different strategies for different components.

With time running out, tough priorities must be set. "Since the 1990s, there has been what I would sum up as mission drift," said Ullas Karanth of the Wildlife Conservation Society, who is one of the world's most respected tiger biologists. Apparently, the drift toward tiger conservation activities like eco-development and social programs—which possibly have greater fund-raising appeal than antipoaching patrols—

takes away funds and energy from the single most vital task: safeguarding core breeding populations of tigers. "If these are lost," Karanth said, "you will have tiger landscapes with no tigers."

Decades of experience and failures have yielded a conservation strategy that, according to Rabinowitz, "allows any site or landscape to increase its tigers if followed correctly." Central to this approach is the need for systematic patrolling and monitoring of sites assessed as harboring defensible core tiger populations. In this way, a population of a mere half dozen breeding females can rebound.[6]

For now, the essential task is to save the few tigers that actually exist. In November 2010—the Year of the Tiger—the world's 13 tiger countries came together at the Global Tiger Summit in St. Petersburg, Russia. Together, they agreed on the need "to double the number of wild tigers across their range by 2022." Most authorities believe that the fight to save the tiger can be won—but that it must be fought with tireless professional focus that keeps to a proven strategy. It will require the human species to display not merely resolve but outright zealotry.[7]

[6]If something rebounds, it successfully goes back to a previous state or level.
[7]If someone displays zealotry, they display very extreme views and behavior.

Adapted from "A Cry for the Tiger," by Caroline Alexander: National Geographic Magazine, December 2011.

Caroline Alexander is the author of several best-selling books, including *The Bounty: The True Story of the Mutiny on the Bounty* (2004), for which she was nominated for the National Book Critic's Circle Award.

A Bengal tiger in the Sundarbans, India, pauses in a river to listen to another tiger's roar.

UNDERSTANDING THE READING

A Check (✓) three statements that best summarize the writer's main ideas.

UNDERSTANDING MAIN IDEAS

☐ 1. Safeguarding main breeding areas should be a top priority for tiger conservation.

☐ 2. It is a positive sign that tigers have been spotted outside of tiger reserves in India.

☐ 3. We should not accept the idea the tiger will continue to be a rare species; it might die out completely.

☐ 4. Patrolling and monitoring core tiger areas can help to increase tiger populations.

☐ 5. The last few decades of tiger conservation strategies have generally been successful.

☐ 6. Establishing land corridors for Indian tigers is probably unrealistic as a long-term strategy.

B Match each question with the correct answer. Three items are extra.

UNDERSTANDING DETAILS

1. When did the world first realize that tigers were endangered? _____

2. How many tigers were estimated to be alive in the early 1980s? _____

3. What percentage of the world's tigers lives in India? _____

4. How many tigers are in Ranthambore? _____

5. Approximately how many tigers in India live outside of tiger reserves? _____

6. What year was the St. Petersburg Global Tiger Summit? _____

7. How many countries have natural tiger habitats? _____

a. 2010

b. 41

c. the 1990s

d. 4,000

e. 1969

f. 1/3

g. 8,000

h. 20 percent

i. 50 percent

j. 13

C Complete the chart with information from the reading.

IDENTIFYING PROBLEMS, REASONS, AND SOLUTIONS

Problem: Tigers are endangered	
Possible Reasons	**Possible Solutions**
Past conservation efforts were not effective	
Growth of human populations	

> **CRITICAL THINKING**   Writers **organize their texts** in specific ways in order to reveal certain information at specific times. Identifying and understanding the organizational structure of a text can help with reading comprehension. The organizational structure can reveal a writer's purpose and point of view. The reader can also anticipate what kind of information might be coming next.

CRITICAL THINKING:
ANALYZING TEXT
ORGANIZATION

D   How does the writer organize the article? Number the ideas in the correct order (1–5).

_____ a. reasons for why tigers have become rare

_____ b. an outline of a variety of global initiatives to save the tiger

_____ c. a description of the power and mystery of tigers

_____ d. a detailed explanation of how one country is trying to protect tiger habitats

_____ e. a description of how urgent it is to save the last remaining tigers

CRITICAL THINKING:
ANALYZING TEXT
ORGANIZATION

E   Discuss the questions with a partner.

1. Do you think the opening of the article is effective? Why or why not?

2. How else could the writer have organized the article?

CRITICAL THINKING:
GUESSING MEANING
FROM CONTEXT

F   Find and underline the following words and phrases in the reading passage. Use the context to help you identify the meaning of each word or phrase. Then match each word or phrase with its definition.

1. Paragraph A: **indifference** _____

2. Paragraph C: **unnerving** _____

3. Paragraph D: **defining attribute** _____

4. Paragraph D: **annihilation** _____

5. Paragraph E: **botched** _____

6. Paragraph E: **dispersed** _____

7. Paragraph G: **unwelcome revelation** _____

8. Paragraph L: **harboring** _____

a. an unpleasant and surprising discovery

b. a key characteristic to someone's identity

c. lack of interest or concern

d. total defeat or destruction

e. spread over a wide area

f. failed; mismanaged

g. giving a safe home or shelter to (something)

h. making (someone) lose courage or confidence

CRITICAL THINKING:
PERSONALIZING

G   How important do you think it is to protect endangered animals? Note your ideas below. Then discuss with a partner.

_____

_____

_____

DEVELOPING READING SKILLS

An appositive is a noun or a noun phrase that explains, defines, or gives more information about another noun or noun phrase that is close to it. Writers use commas, dashes, or colons to separate appositives from the nouns that they describe. For example, the underlined phrases in the sentences below are appositives. The double-underlined words are the nouns that they describe.

"I've never met a head of state who says, 'Look, we're a poor country. If it comes between tigers and people, you just have to write off tigers,'" said <u>Alan Rabinowitz, an authority on tigers and the CEO of Panthera</u>.

A spiderweb of green lines weaves among core tiger populations, forming a network that includes breathtaking <u>extremes of habitat—Himalayan foothills, jungle, swamp, forest, grasslands</u>.

Long-term conservation must focus on all aspects of <u>a tiger landscape: core breeding populations, sanctuaries, wildlife corridors, and the surrounding human communities</u>.

A In each of these sentences from the passage, underline the appositive and circle the noun or noun phrase that it refers to. One sentence has two noun phrase appositives that refer to two different nouns.

UNDERSTANDING APPOSITIVES

1. My determination to see a wild tiger in my lifetime brought me to Ranthambore Tiger Reserve, one of 40 in India.

2. "This is about making decisions as if we're in an emergency room," says Tom Kaplan, co-founder of Panthera, an organization dedicated to big cats.

3. The places that have actual tigers—here-and-now, flesh-and-blood tigers—as opposed to hypothetical ones, are represented by a scattering of brown-colored spots.

4. Over the next decade, infrastructure projects—the kind of development that often destroys habitat—are projected to average some $750 billion a year in Asia.

5. In November 2010—the Year of the Tiger—the world's 13 tiger countries came together at the Global Tiger Summit in St. Petersburg, Russia.

B Scan for and underline other examples of appositives in the reading passage in Unit 1. Share your answers with a partner.

APPLYING

A pair of Siberian tiger cubs

TIGERS IN THE SNOW

BEFORE VIEWING

DISCUSSION

A What threats to tigers do you remember from the reading? Make a list.

_____

_____

LEARNING ABOUT THE TOPIC

B Read the information. Then answer the questions.

Siberian (or Amur) tigers live mainly in the forests of Russia's far east, though some still exist in China and North Korea. The climates that these tigers live in are harsh—temperatures in some areas can drop to −40°C—but this also offers some advantages. These cold northern forests offer the lowest human density of any tiger habitat, allowing the tigers far more room to move around. However, the Siberian tiger, like other tiger species, is endangered. Estimates suggest that there are fewer than 500 individuals left in Russia.

1. In what kind of areas do Siberian tigers live? What advantages do these areas offer the tigers?

_____

_____

2. Why do you think Siberian tigers might be endangered?

_____

C Read these extracts from the video. Match the correct form of each **bold** word to its definition.

> "Once the kill has been made, it's clear the male is the **dominant** partner. He won't allow the female to get near until he's had enough."
>
> "They are at the top of their **food chain**, but the tigers are still endangered."
>
> "It is thought its fragile population has been **stabilized** for the moment."

1. _____ (v) to get to a state in which there aren't any more big problems or changes

2. _____ (adj) more powerful, successful, influential, or noticeable than others

3. _____ (n) the process by which one living thing is eaten by another, which is then eaten by another, and so on

WHILE VIEWING

A ▶ Watch the video. Check the main idea.

☐ a. Siberian tigers are in danger, but their populations are currently remaining steady.

☐ b. Siberian tigers are in danger, and their populations are decreasing very quickly.

☐ c. Siberian tigers were endangered, but their populations are now getting bigger.

B ▶ Watch the video again. Then answer the questions below.

1. How is a Siberian tiger different from other tigers?

   _____

2. How big does a Siberian tiger's territory have to be?

   Female: _____   Male: _____

3. According to the video, what are the two main threats to Siberian tigers?

   _____

4. How has the Siberian tiger's decline changed since the mid-1990s?

   _____

AFTER VIEWING

A Why do you think male tigers need such a large home range? Note your ideas below. Then discuss with a partner.

_____

B How does the Siberian tiger's situation compare with the challenges facing other tigers? Note your ideas below. Then discuss with a partner.

_____

_____

Writing

EXPLORING WRITTEN ENGLISH

VOCABULARY FOR WRITING

A The following words and expressions can be useful when writing about problems and solutions. Use the words to complete the definitions.

> **threatened** (paragraph D)　　**exacerbated** (paragraph E)　**sacrifice** (paragraph I)
>
> **initiatives** (paragraph J)　　**funding** (paragraph J)　　　**components** (paragraph J)
>
> **safeguarding** (paragraph K)　**strategy** (paragraph L)

1. _____ is money that a government or organization provides for a particular purpose.

2. If an animal species is _____, it is likely to become endangered.

3. _____ are parts or elements of a larger whole.

4. If something _____ a problem or bad situation, it made it worse.

5. _____ are important actions that are intended to solve a particular problem.

6. _____ something is keeping it from harm or danger.

7. A(n) _____ is a plan of action designed to achieve a long-term or overall aim.

8. If you _____ something that is valuable or important, you give it up, usually to obtain something else for yourself or for other people.

A critically endangered female Sumatran tiger and her five-month-old cub

B Read the information in the box. Then use appositives to combine the sentence pairs (1–5).

LANGUAGE FOR WRITING Using Appositives

As you saw in the Reading Skill section, writers use appositives to give more information about a noun. Appositives help writers avoid redundancy and short, choppy sentences. You can separate appositives with commas, dashes, or colons.

With an appositive:
"I've never met a head of state who says, 'Look, we're a poor country. If it comes between tigers and people, you just have to write off tigers,'" said Alan Rabinowitz, <u>a renowned authority on tigers and the CEO of Panthera</u>.

Without an appositive:
"I've never met a head of state who says, 'Look, we're a poor country. If it comes between tigers and people, you just have to write off tigers,'" said Alan Rabinowitz. Rabinowitz is a renowned authority on tigers and the CEO of Panthera.

---

1. The Bengal tiger is one of India's most popular attractions. The Bengal tiger is India's national animal.

   _____

   _____

2. In addition to tigers, other animals live in Ranthambore. Monkeys, deer, wild boars, owls, and parakeets live in Ranthambore.

   _____

   _____

3. Ranthambore is home to 41 tigers. Ranthambore is a former private hunting estate.

   _____

   _____

4. Fateh Singh Rathore used to work at Ranthambore when it was a hunting estate. Fateh Singh Rathore is the assistant field director of the reserve.

   _____

   _____

5. Zaw Win Khaing once saw a tiger in 2002. Zaw Win Khaing is the head ranger of a tiger reserve in Myanmar.

   _____

   _____

Individual paragraphs have main ideas. Similarly, essays have main ideas. A **thesis statement** is a statement that expresses the main idea of an entire essay. A good thesis statement has the following characteristics:

- It presents your position or opinion on the topic.

- It includes a reference to the reasons for your opinion or position on the topic.

- It expresses only the ideas that you can easily explain in your body paragraphs.

CRITICAL THINKING: EVALUATING

C Read the following pairs of thesis statements. Check (✓) the statement in each pair that you think is better. Then share your answers with a partner.

1. a. ☐ Palisades Park should be protected for three main reasons: It is the only park in the city, it is a gathering place for families, and it is a safe place for children to play after school.

   b. ☐ Palisades Park is a beautiful place for parents to spend time with their children and for people in the community to gather for events.

2. a. ☐ The Bloodroot plant (*Sanguinaria Canadensis*) is endangered and should be protected because it can cure dozens of ailments, from skin disorders to cancer.

   b. ☐ The Bloodroot plant (*Sanguinaria Canadensis*), an endangered plant found in the forests of North America, can be used to cure diseases.

A bloodroot plant

CRITICAL THINKING: EVALUATING

D Read the question below about tiger conservation. Write your opinion and two reasons. Then use your opinion and your reasons to write a thesis statement.

Should governments spend more money to protect tigers?

My opinion: _____

_____

Reason 1: _____

_____

Reason 2: _____

_____

Thesis statement: _____

_____

_____

WRITING TASK

> **GOAL** You are going to write an essay on the following topic:
>
> Describe an animal, a habitat, or a natural place that people are working to protect. Explain why it should be protected.

A Make a list of animals, habitats, or natural places that people are trying to protect. If you need more ideas, go online and research.

BRAINSTORMING

B Follow the steps to make notes for your essay.

PLANNING

    Step 1 Choose one idea to write about from your brainstorming list.

    Step 2 Complete the outline below with notes about the idea. Go online to do some research if you need more information.

OUTLINE

Introduction

Information about the animal/habitat/place: _____

_____

_____

How is it valuable? _____

Why is it in danger? _____

Thesis statement: We need to protect _____

because _____ and _____.

Body paragraph 1

Topic sentence: (Reason 1) _____

Supporting detail: _____

Supporting detail: _____

Body paragraph 2

Topic sentence: (Reason 2) _____

_____

Supporting detail: _____

Supporting detail: _____

Conclusion

What can be done to protect it? _____

_____

_____

REVISING PRACTICE

The draft below is a model of the essay you are writing. Follow the steps to create a better second draft.

1. Add the sentences (a–c) in the most suitable spaces.

   a. With a combination of international and local efforts, Borneo may be saved from destruction.

   b. so that we can save all the different forms of life that live on the island.

   c. because it is home to so many different species and because the rain forest helps reverse damage from climate change.

2. Now fix the following problems (a–c) with the essay.

   a. Cross out one sentence that doesn't relate to the topic of the essay in paragraph B.

   b. Use an appositive to revise the first two sentences in paragraph C.

   c. Use an appositive to revise sentences five and six in paragraph D.

A

The rain forest island of Borneo, the world's third largest island, is about the size of the state of Texas in the United States. The island is one of the most biodiverse places in the world. It is home to endangered animals such as the Sumatran tiger, the Sumatran rhinoceros, the pygmy elephant, and the Bornean orangutan. And nearly 400 new species have been discovered in 10 years. Sadly, this island's diverse and beautiful rain forest is in danger. In the past 20 years, 80 percent of the rain forest has been destroyed because of illegal logging, forest fires, and development. At the same time, people are capturing and selling some of the wildlife, particularly the orangutans. We need to protect Borneo _____

B

It's important to protect Borneo _____. Visitors to Borneo can enjoy its beautiful beaches and mountains. Thousands of species of plants, animals, and insects live on Borneo. Many, like the pygmy elephant, cannot be found anywhere else on Earth. In addition, scientists continue to find new species of plants and animals. Some of these might provide medicines for diseases or teach us more about biology.

C

We also need to protect Borneo in order to protect the globe from climate change. Borneo is home of one of the world's remaining rain forests. Carbon dioxide, a greenhouse gas, is heating up Earth's atmosphere and causing a number of problems such as extreme weather and melting polar ice. Rain forests absorb carbon dioxide and create more oxygen. They also help produce rain all around the world. If we lose rain forests, we will lose one of our best weapons against global warming.

D

So, what can be done to protect Borneo? Both international and local communities are involved in saving the island. An organization called the World Wildlife Fund (WWF) is working to create safety corridors and protect the 220,000-square-kilometer (85,000-square-mile) area from destruction. The organization is raising funds to help make this happen. The Borneo Project is an international organization. The Borneo Project provides support to local communities. These communities protect the rain forests of Borneo in various ways: They stop loggers from cutting down trees, they educate the local community about the need to save the rain forest, and they block developers from building on the land. _____

D Now use the questions below to revise your essay.

☐ Does your introduction have an interesting hook?

☐ Does your thesis state your position on the topic?

☐ Do your body paragraphs include enough details to fully explain your ideas?

☐ Did you use appositives to avoid redundancy and short, choppy sentences?

☐ Do all your sentences relate to the main idea?

☐ Does your concluding paragraph have a summary statement and a final thought?

Orangutans in a Borneo forest sanctuary

EDITING PRACTICE

Read the information below. Then find and correct one mistake with appositives in each of the sentences (1–5).

In sentences with appositives, remember that an appositive must:
- be a noun or a noun phrase.
- come right after a noun or noun phrase.
- be separated by commas, dashes, or colons.

1. Tigers, they are an endangered species, live throughout Asia.

2. Ranthambore, a tiger reserve is in India.

3. Tiger conservationists—people who protect tigers, are looking for new solutions.

4. Corridors, are paths for safe travel, may help tigers survive in wild areas.

5. There are fewer than 4,000 tigers. The biggest cat in the world.

FINAL DRAFT   **E**   **Follow the steps to write a final draft.**

1. Check your revised draft for mistakes with appositives.

2. Now use the checklist on page 248 to write a final draft. Make any other necessary changes.

UNIT REVIEW
Answer the following questions.

1. What are two reasons tigers are endangered?

_____

_____

2. What are two ways we can help protect tigers?

_____

_____

3. What are two things a thesis statement should include?

_____

_____

4. Do you remember the meanings of these words? Check (✓) the ones you know. Look back at the unit and review the ones you don't know.

☐ acknowledge AWL   ☐ poaching

☐ apparently AWL   ☐ predator

☐ assess AWL   ☐ prey

☐ authority AWL   ☐ priority AWL

☐ dedicated   ☐ project AWL

☐ feasible   ☐ resolve AWL

☐ hypothetical AWL   ☐ secretive

☐ lethal

BEAUTY AND PERCEPTION

3

A visitor looks at artwork during an art festival at the Dubai World Trade Center.

ok at the information on these pages and answer the questions.

What is *aesthetics*?

According to the text, what factors affect aesthetic principles?

Is the image on the opposite page beautiful, in your opinion? If so, what makes it beautiful?

atch the correct form of the words in blue to their definitions.

_____ (n) the basic rules or laws of a particular theory

_____ (n) the size of something or its size in relation to other things

_____ (adj) relating to patterns and shapes with regular lines

WHAT IS BEAUTY?

Aesthetics is a branch of philosophy concerned with the study of beauty. Aesthetic **principles** provide a set of criteria for creating and evaluating artistic objects such as sculptures and paintings, as well as music, film, and other art forms.

Aesthetic principles have existed almost as long as people have been producing art. Aesthetics were especially important to the ancient Greeks, whose principles have had a great influence on Western art. The Greeks believed that beautiful objects were intrinsically beautiful; that is, their beauty did not depend on people's interpretation of them. Concepts such as **proportion**, symmetry, and order made objects beautiful.

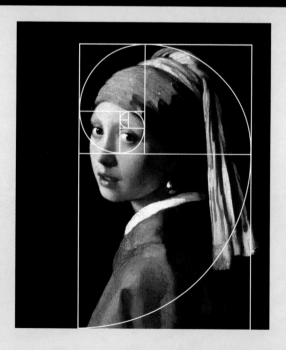

Today, however, most people would agree that

Johannes Vermeer's
Girl with a Pearl Earring

Reading

PREPARING TO READ

BUILDING
VOCABULARY

A The words in **blue** below are used in the reading passage. Match the correct form of each word to its definition (1–8).

The time and place in which a work of art is created often influence its aesthetic value. Therefore, understanding the historical and social **context** of a work of art can help you to appreciate it better and give you **insight** into its significance. For example, many works of European and American art during the mid- to late 19th century have Asian—or more specifically, Japanese—influences.

Artists such as Vincent van Gogh and James McNeill Whistler incorporated into their own work the subjects, colors, and **composition** of Japanese prints. They were **exposed to** Japanese art partly because Japan opened up to the West in the mid-1800s. As a result, European exhibitions started showing art objects from Japan. Artists who were looking for new styles were especially influenced by Japanese woodblock prints, which **violated** the rules of traditional Western art. To Western eyes, objects in Japanese woodblock prints look flat instead of three-dimensional. Scenes do not have perspective, as in Western paintings.

There were other **crucial** elements that pointed to the differences in Western and Asian **notions** of beauty. For example, the arrangement of objects in Japanese prints is often irregular and asymmetrical, and the focal point—the central object in a print—is often off center, not in the middle as in a Western painting. Some artists were so inspired by these new ideas that they even moved to Japan during the late 19th century in order to **pursue** their interest in Asian art.

▶ *Sudden Shower Over Shin-Ohashi Bridge and Atake,* **by Hiroshige (left), and** *Bridge in the Rain (after Hiroshige),* **by Vincent Van Gogh**

1. _____ (v) to follow

2. _____ (v) to bring into contact with

3. _____ (adj) extremely important

4. _____ (n) the general situation that an idea or an event relates to

5. _____ (n) an accurate and deep understanding of something

6. _____ (v) to break or to fail to comply with

7. _____ (n) ideas or beliefs about something

8. _____ (n) the way in which the parts of something are arranged

B Complete the sentences with the words in the box. Use a dictionary to help you. BUILDING VOCABULARY

balance	depression	ethics	imperfect

1. _____ is a mental state in which you are sad and feel that you cannot enjoy anything.

2. _____ are ideas or moral beliefs that influence the behavior, attitudes, or philosophy of a group of people.

3. If something has _____, elements in it are treated equally in terms of strength or importance.

4. If a thing is _____, it has faults; it is missing certain possible desirable qualities or characteristics.

C Discuss these questions with a partner. USING VOCABULARY

1. What skills do you think are **crucial** if you want to be a professional artist?

2. Would you encourage someone with artistic talent to **pursue** a career in art? Why or why not?

D Discuss your answer to this question in small groups: Look at the everyday items around you. Can you see anything beautiful? What makes it beautiful to you? BRAINSTORMING

_____

_____

E Look at the photos in the reading passage and read the first sentence of each paragraph. What are some of the aspects of photography that the reading passage discusses? Note your ideas below. Then read the passage to check your answers. PREVIEWING

_____

_____

_____

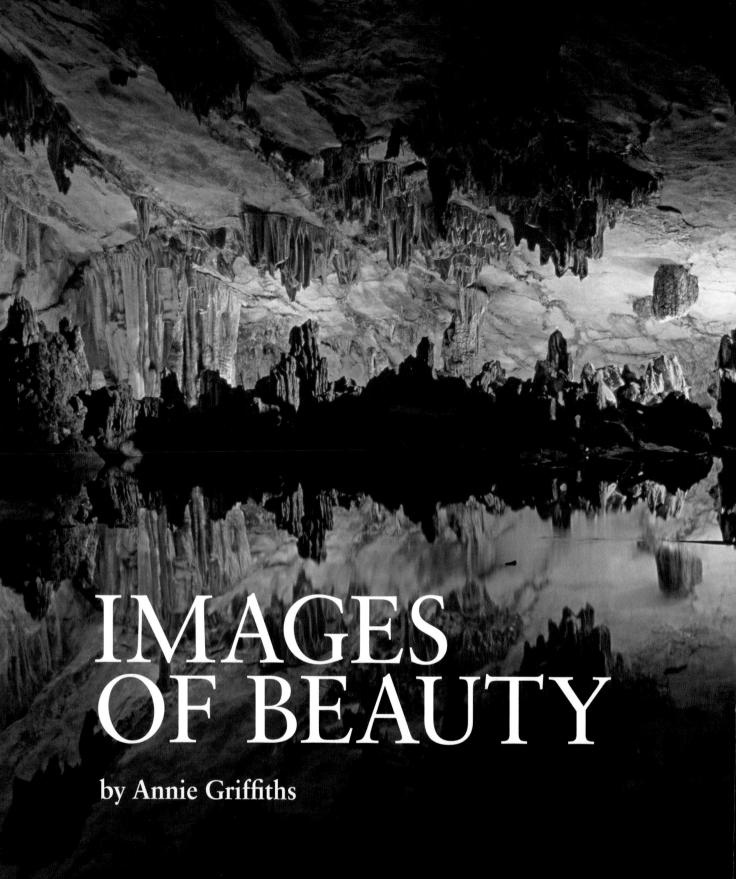

IMAGES
OF BEAUTY

by Annie Griffiths

**Reed Flute Cave, China,
by Raymond Gehman**

> Some photographs rise above the others. These are photos that catch a moment of emotion or light that make them ignite a deeper response in the viewer.

🎧 1.3

Photography has opened our eyes to a multitude of beauties, things we literally could not have seen before the advent of the frozen image. It has greatly expanded our **notion** of what is beautiful, what is aesthetically pleasing. Items formerly considered trivial, and not worth an artist's paint, have been revealed and honored by photographs: things as pedestrian as a fence post, a chair, a vegetable. And as technology has developed, photographers have explored completely new points of view: those of the microscope, the eagle, the cosmos.

What is it that delights the human eye and allows us to proclaim that a photograph is beautiful? Photography depends on three **principles**: light, **composition**, and moment. Light literally makes the recording of an image possible, but in the right hands, light in a photograph can make the image soar. The same is true with composition. What the photographer chooses to keep in or out of the frame is all that we will ever see—but that combination is vital. And the moment that the shutter is pressed, when an instant is frozen in time, endows[1] the whole image with meaning. When the three—light, composition, and moment—are in concert, there is visual magic.

Let us begin with light. Light literally reveals the subject. Without light, there is nothing: no sight, no color, no form. How light is **pursued** and captured is the photographer's constant challenge and constant joy. We watch it dance across a landscape or a face, and we prepare for the moment when it illuminates or softens or ignites the subject before us. Light is rarely interesting when it is flawless. Photographers may be the only people at the beach or on the mountaintop praying for clouds, because nothing condemns a photograph more than a blazingly bright sky. Light is usually best when it is fleeting or dappled,[2] razor sharp or threatening, or atmospheric. On a physiological level, we are all solar powered. Scientific studies have proved that our moods are profoundly affected by the amount of light we are **exposed** to. Lack of sun has been linked to loss of energy and even **depression**. Light in a photograph sets an emotional expectation. It can be soft or harsh, broad or delicate, but the mood that light sets is

---

[1]If you **endow** something with a particular feature or quality, you provide it with that feature or quality.

[2]**Dappled** light is a combination of dark and light patches on the object or person that is being illuminated.

a preface to the whole image. Consider the light in a stunning scene by Sam Abell (below). It is the quality of light through morning fog that blesses this image and turns a forest into a field of light, shadow, and color, where every tree takes on a personality.

Composition represents the structural choices the photographer makes within the photographic frame. Everything in the photo can either contribute or distract. Ironically, the definition of what makes a picture aesthetically pleasing often comes down to mathematics: the geometric **proportions** of objects and their placements within the frame. When we look at a beautiful photograph with an objective eye, we can often

D find serpentine³ lines, figure eights, and triangular arrangements formed by the objects. The **balance**, or mathematical proportion, of the objects makes up the picture's composition: a key element in any beautiful image. Look closely at photographer James Stanfield's charming composition of a child jumping for joy in a doorway at the Louvre (right). It is the moment that draws us in, but that moment is set in a striking composition of the doorway and the architecture beyond. The

³Something that is **serpentine** is curving and winding in shape, like a snake.

geometric composition of the photograph makes the child look small, and even more appealing.

The third **crucial** element in a photograph is the moment when the shutter is pressed. The moment captured in a beautiful image is the storytelling part of the photograph. Whether a small gesture or a grand climax, it is the moment within a picture that draws us in and makes us care. It may be the photographer's most important choice. If a special moment is caught, it endows the whole

E image with meaning. Often, waiting for that moment involves excruciating patience, as the photographer anticipates that something miraculous is about to happen. At other times, it's an almost electric reaction that seems to bypass the thought process entirely and fire straight to instinct. Capturing that perfect moment may be a photographer's biggest challenge, because most important moments are fleeting. Hands touch. The ball drops. A smile flashes. Miss the moment and it is gone forever.

Light, composition, and moment are the basic elements in any beautiful photograph. But there

F are three other elements that draw the viewer in and encourage an emotional response. These are palette, time, and wonder.

Morning fog at Kelly's Ford, Virginia, United States, by Sam Abell

re, Paris,
eld

BEAUTY AND PERCEPTION

Palette refers to the selection of colors in a photograph that create a visual **context**. Colors can range from neon to a simple gradation of grays in a black-and-white photograph. Even in the abstract, colors can make us feel elated or sad. The chosen palette sets up the mood of the whole image. It can invite or repel, soothe or agitate. We feel calm in a palette of pastels. Icy blues can make us shiver. Oranges and reds tend to energize.

Other images stand out because of the freezing or blurring of time. There are the lovely images of raindrops falling, lightning flashing, and athletes frozen in midair. There are also time exposures[4] that allow us to see a choreography of movement within the still frame. The laundry flutters, the traffic merges, the water flows. In a photograph of a bird in flight, the high-speed exposure allows us to see things that our eyes literally cannot: every feather supporting the bird's flight, the arc of the wings, the light in the bird's eye. High-speed photography has been a gift to both art and science.

[4]A **time exposure** is a photograph that results when the camera's shutter is left open for a long time.

Wonder refers to the measure of human response when the photograph reveals something extraordinary—something never seen before, or seen in a fresh, new way. Wonder is about **insight** and curiosity. It is an expression of the child inside every one of us. Some photographers, following their childlike sense of wonder, have literally given their lives in pursuit of images so wonderful that they must be seen.

Light, composition, and moment come together in a photograph to bring us the ultimate reality: a view of the world unknown before the invention of the camera. Before photography, the basic artistic rules of painting were rarely **violated**. Images were made to please, not to capture reality. But as photography evolved, painterly[5] rules were often rejected in the pursuit of fresh vision. Photographers became interested in the real world, warts and all, and it was the accidental detail that was celebrated. Photography invited the world to see with new eyes—to see photographically—and all of the arts benefited from this new point of view.

[5]**Painterly** means relating to or characteristic of painting or painters.

An aerial view of the towering Kronotsky volcano, Kamchatka, Russia, by Michael Melford

Time exposure of cars speeding past a cowboy on horseback, Badlands, United States, by Annie Griffiths

Painters, sculptors, designers, weavers, and dancers all expanded their vision of beauty by embracing the photographer's love of reality. And when the photographer is creative with the basic elements in a photograph, the resulting image has greater appeal. A surprising truth about photography is that each element is most effective not when it captures perfection but rather when it reveals the **imperfect**. Photographs are most eloquent when they impart a new way of seeing. What is more wonderful than the imperfect moment, when a simple scene turns sublime[6] because a cat entered the room, the mirror caught a reflection, or a shaft of light came through the window? And real beauty depends upon how the image moves us: A photograph can make us care, understand, react, emote,[7] and empathize with the wider world by humanizing and honoring the unknown.

Photographs have created a new **ethic** of seeing. They have greatly expanded our notion of what is beautiful. It is to photography's credit that it has found beauty in the most humble places, and that it has ushered in a new democracy of vision. People from all walks of life are able to feast their eyes on subjects remote and grand. Photographs have given us visual proof that the world is grander than we imagined, that there is beauty, often overlooked, in nearly everything.

Adapted from "Simply Beautiful Photographs" by Annie Griffiths: National Geographic Books, 2010

[6]If you describe something as **sublime**, you mean that it has a wonderful quality that affects you deeply.

[7]To **emote** is to express emotion in an intense way.

Photographer and writer Annie Griffiths has documented the lives of people in nearly 150 countries around the world. She has received awards from the National Press Photographers Association, the Associated Press, and the White House News Photographers Association.

UNDERSTANDING THE READING

A Note answers to the questions below.

1. What are the three main elements that make a photograph beautiful?

   _____

2. What additional elements make a photograph beautiful?

   _____

3. The passage is divided into two main parts. Which paragraph begins the second part?

   _____

B Note answers to the questions below. Then discuss with a partner.

1. How has photography changed our notion of beauty?

   _____

   _____

2. Write a definition for each of the main elements you listed in exercise A, question 1.

   _____

   _____

   _____

3. What is the effect of color in a photograph, according to Griffiths?

   _____

   _____

4. What kinds of things do time exposures help us to see in a photograph?

   _____

   _____

5. What is wonder as it applies to a photograph, according to Griffiths? Explain it in your own words.

   _____

   _____

6. How has photography affected other art forms?

   _____

   _____

> **CRITICAL THINKING** **Applying ideas** from a reading to other contexts can help you evaluate the information. For example, applying an author's opinion to your own experience can help you decide how far you agree with it.

C Find the following quotes in paragraph J of the reading passage. Note answers to the questions. Then discuss with a partner.

1. "Before photography, the basic artistic rules of painting were rarely violated. Images were made to please, not to capture reality." Can you think of any famous paintings or types of artwork that are examples of this idea?

_____

_____

2. "A surprising truth about photography is that each element is most effective not when it captures perfection but rather when it reveals the imperfect." Can you find a picture in this book that is an example of this? Do you agree with the writer?

_____

_____

D Find and underline the *italicized* words below in the passage. Use the context to help you understand the meaning. Then circle the correct words to complete the definitions.

1. Paragraph A: If something is *pedestrian*, it's **ordinary** / **extraordinary**.
2. Paragraph B: You use *in concert* when you're talking about things that **work well together** / **are not coordinated**.
3. Paragraph D: If an idea *comes down to* something in particular, it means it is an **essential** / **unimportant** part of it.
4. Paragraph E: If a moment is *fleeting*, it goes by very **slowly** / **quickly**.
5. Paragraph J: If a photograph shows images of real life, *warts and all*, then it is showing us **just the positive** / **both the positive and the negative** aspects of reality.
6. Paragraph K: If something has *ushered in* a thing, such as a new era or way of thinking, it has **ended it** / **brought it into being**.
7. Paragraph K: People from *all walks of life* are people who come from **similar** / **different** backgrounds.

E What is your opinion of the photograph below? Consider the elements of a beautiful photograph mentioned in the reading passage. Discuss with a partner.

Argentine gauchos photographed by O. Louis Mazzatenta

DEVELOPING READING SKILLS

> **READING SKILL** Using a Concept Map to Identify Supporting Details
>
> A **concept map** is a type of graphic organizer. It helps you see how main ideas and details in a reading passage relate to each other. Taking notes in a concept map can help you understand and remember information so you can use it later in a discussion, a writing assignment, or a test.
>
> When you take notes in any kind of graphic organizer, be as brief as possible. Use abbreviations and leave out unimportant or repeated information.

USING A
CONCEPT MAP

A Complete the concept map using information from the reading passage.

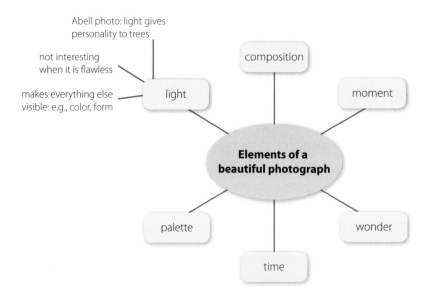

USING A
CONCEPT MAP

B Now look back at the reading passage in Unit 1. Create a concept map to summarize the key ideas relating to the Anthropocene.

Video

PHOTO CONTEST

"A Node in the Dark,"
by Brian Yen

BEFORE VIEWING

A How would you rate the photo above? Consider Griffiths's six criteria and discuss in a small group.

DISCUSSION

_____

_____

B Read the information. Then answer the questions.

LEARNING ABOUT
THE TOPIC

Each year, National Geographic invites amateur photographers to enter their photographs into a competition. In 2014, people from more than 150 countries submitted photos representing three categories: people, places, and nature. Over 9,000 photos were submitted, but only a handful were chosen as winners. The winning entries all had one thing in common: they told a story. The grand prize winner, Brian Yen, received $10,000 and a trip to National Geographic headquarters. When asked why he takes pictures, he explained, "Photography to me is like going on an archaeological dig: It offers me a tool to interpret reality by dusting away the uninteresting bits to reveal the gem underneath. It's an exciting, creative, and exploratory process. "

1. What story does Yen's photo tell?

_____

2. Why does Yen compare taking pictures to archaeology?

_____

C Read these extracts from the video. Match the correct form of each **bold** word to its definition.

> "Everyone looks really peaceful but at the same time it just looks really **surreal** and something, you know, otherworldly."
>
> "The overall **tone** of it was just very relaxing in what was a very **chaotic** scene."
>
> "A photograph like this has got to be like a chessboard, where everything is there and there's no **foreground**."

1. _____ (adj) strange; dreamlike

2. _____ (adj) not having any order or organization

3. _____ (n) the front part of a picture

4. _____ (v) the general character or feeling of something, for example a place or piece of writing

WHILE VIEWING

A ▶ Watch the video about judging the 2014 National Geographic Photo Contest. What criteria for judging the photos do the judges mention?

A winning photo …
- ☐ a. should have just one main element.
- ☐ b. touches the viewer emotionally.
- ☐ c. must be good technically.
- ☐ d. must have good composition.
- ☐ e. needs to look natural.
- ☐ f. has good use of color and light.
- ☐ g. shows something new and unusual.

B ▶ Watch the video again. Match each image from the video (a–e) with a statement.

a. the swimming pool   b. the owl   c. the wildebeest   d. the train   e. the basketball game

1. It took time for the judges to appreciate it. _____

2. The judges had divided opinions about it. _____

3. A judge felt that it offered a new perspective. _____

4. The judges felt it had a calming effect on them. _____

5. It was rejected by the judging panel. _____

AFTER VIEWING

A What do you think the judge means when he refers to a "gut reaction"? Discuss with a partner.

B Considering the elements of a good photo described earlier, which photo in the video do you think was best? Discuss your choice with a partner.

_____

_____

Writing

EXPLORING WRITTEN ENGLISH

A The following words and expressions can be useful when writing about visual art forms. Find the words in this unit's reading passage. Use the context to guess their meanings. Then use the words to complete the definitions.

VOCABULARY FOR WRITING

> **aesthetically pleasing** (paragraph A)   **within the frame** (paragraph D)
> **illuminate** (paragraph C)   **gradation** (paragraph G)
> **atmospheric** (paragraph C)   **pastels** (paragraph G)

1. If a scene is _____, it creates a pleasant mood or feeling.

2. If a work of art is _____, it is beautiful.

3. In a photograph, things that are _____ are the things that the photographer has chosen to include in the image.

4. To _____ something means to shine light on it.

5. A(n) _____ is a small change in something, such as a slight change from one color to another.

6. _____ are pale colors.

B Read the sentences (a–e) below. Then answer the questions (1–3).

NOTICING

a. The winning photo was taken by Brian Yen, <u>who lives in Hong Kong</u>.

b. My personal favorite was the photo <u>that came in second place</u>.

c. Yen's photo, <u>which is called "A Node Glows in the Dark,"</u> uses an interesting balance of light and dark.

d. Yen, <u>whose image shows people on a train at night</u>, mostly takes photos after dark.

e. The central focus of the image is on the woman <u>who is using her cellphone</u>.

1. What is the purpose of the underlined clauses?

   _____

2. What words are used to introduce the underlined clauses?

   _____

3. If you take away the underlined clauses, which sentences still make sense? Why?

   _____

Writers use adjective clauses to give more information about nouns. An adjective clause has a subject and a verb.

*Palette is a term **that** refers to the selection of colors in a photograph.*

*My father was someone **who** was interested in photography from a young age.*

As in the examples above, restrictive adjective clauses give essential information about a noun. In other words, if you take away the clause, the sentence no longer makes sense. Nonrestrictive adjective clauses give nonessential information:

*Our concept of beauty has been influenced by photography, **which** is a relatively recent art form.*

*Annie Griffiths, **who** is a professional photographer, is the executive director of an organization that empowers women in developing countries.*

*Annie Leibovitz, **whose** photographs have been published in several magazines, is famous for her use of light and color.*

Adjective clauses are a good way to add details to your writing. They help vary your sentence types and make your sentences more interesting.

Note: Remember to use commas in nonrestrictive adjective clauses. Use one comma before a nonrestrictive adjective clause that appears at the end of a sentence. Use commas before and after a nonrestrictive adjective clause when it appears in the middle of a sentence. Use *which* (not *that*) for objects in nonrestrictive adjective clauses.

C Read the pairs of sentences below. Join them into a single sentence using a restrictive or nonrestrictive adjective clause.

1. Vivian Maier was a photographer. Her work was only discovered after her death.

   _____

   _____

2. Ansel Adams was an American photographer. He was most known for his images of the Californian wilderness.

   _____

   _____

3. Aesthetics were important to the ancient Greeks. They believed beautiful objects were intrinsically beautiful.

   _____

   _____

4. Vincent van Gogh was influenced by Japanese art. He made a copy of Hiroshige's print *Sudden Storm Over Shin-Ohashi Bridge and Atake.*

   _____

   _____

D Write three sentences about photographs in this unit using nonrestrictive or restrictive adjective clauses.

- _____
  _____

- _____
  _____

- _____
  _____

WRITING SKILL Supporting a Thesis

As you saw in Unit 2, a thesis statement expresses the main idea of an entire essay. Each body paragraph in an essay then provides details for and explanation of the main idea. To effectively support a thesis statement, make sure you do the following:

- Describe one key point of your thesis in the topic sentence of each body paragraph.
- Order your body paragraphs to match the order of ideas mentioned in your thesis statement.
- Provide adequate details (facts and examples) that develop the idea of each topic sentence.

E Read this excerpt from an introduction to an essay on Frank Lloyd Wright's famous building, Fallingwater. Underline the key concepts in the thesis statement. Then answer the questions.

CRITICAL THINKING: ANALYZING

The term *organic architecture*, which was coined by the American architect Frank Lloyd Wright, applies to structures that create a sense of harmony with the natural world. Fallingwater, the western Pennsylvania house designed by Wright, is a perfect example of the organic approach to architecture due to its surroundings and its materials.

⎤ **Thesis Statement**

1. How many body paragraphs do you think the essay will have? _____

2. What ideas do you think will appear in the body paragraphs?

_____

_____

_____

_____

F Read the topic sentences below for the essay about Fallingwater. Underline the ideas in the topic sentences that match the main points of the thesis statement.

Body paragraph 1:

Topic sentence: The way Fallingwater is assimilated into its natural environment is an example of organic architecture.

Body paragraph 2:

Topic sentence: The organic approach is also shown in the natural materials Wright used to build Fallingwater.

APPLYING **G** Now read some notes for the essay. Which body paragraph from exercise **F** does each note best support? Match a paragraph (1–2) with each note.

Notes:

_____ a. exterior color matches color of leaves on surrounding plants

_____ b. natural spring drips water into house

_____ c. built from stones found in local area

_____ d. living room fireplace incorporates boulders from a nearby building site

_____ e. house is built around a tree

_____ f. large window in living room overlooks a waterfall

Fallingwater, designed by Frank Lloyd Wright

WRITING TASK

GOAL In this lesson, you are going to write an essay on the following topic:

Choose an example of a visual art form (e.g., a painting, a photograph, a piece of sculpture) and evaluate it using aesthetic criteria.

BRAINSTORMING

A Choose a type of visual art (painting, drawing, photography, sculpture). Think of three criteria to judge it.

Type of art: _____

Criteria: 1. _____   2. _____   3. _____

Now pick one example of your chosen type of visual art. Describe it, and evaluate it based on your criteria.

Name of piece of art: _____

Description	Evaluation
	1.
	2.
	3.

PLANNING

B Follow the steps to make notes for your essay.

Step 1 In the outline on the next page, write a thesis statement and note some ideas for your introduction.

Step 2 Write a topic sentence and two or three details for each body paragraph.

Step 3 Note some ideas for your conclusion.

OUTLINE

Notes for introduction: _____

_____

Thesis statement: _____

_____

Body paragraph 1: Topic sentence: _____

_____

Details: _____

_____

_____

Body paragraph 2: Topic sentence: _____

_____

Details: _____

_____

_____

Body paragraph 3: Topic sentence: _____

Details: _____

_____

_____

Notes for conclusion: _____

_____

FIRST DRAFT **C** Use the information in your outline to write a first draft of your essay.

REVISING PRACTICE

The draft on the next page is an essay that uses a set of criteria to evaluate a building. Follow the steps to create a better second draft.

1. Write the sentences (a–c) in the correct spaces.

   a. For example, it has large double doors that are at street level; there are no stairs at the entrance.
   b. The copper color offers an interesting contrast to the light gray color of the granite structure, and the contrast will remain as the copper ages.
   c. For example, it is resistant to acid rain.

2. Now fix the following problems (a–c) with the essay.

   a. Fix a problem with a nonrestrictive clause in paragraph B.
   b. Fix a problem with a nonrestrictive clause in paragraph D.
   c. Delete an unrelated idea in paragraph D.

A

What makes a work of architecture great? Most people would say that aesthetics are most important. For example, many people agree that the Eiffel Tower in Paris and the Blue Mosque in Istanbul are beautiful structures. It is true that aesthetics are important; however, according to the Roman architect Marcus Vitruvius Pollio, there are two additional principles that we should consider when judging a structure. They are durability—how strong and long-lasting a structure is designed to be—and function—how well the structure serves its intended purpose. The new Rostonville Library in my city is a good example of Vitruvius's principles because it is durable, functional, and aesthetically pleasing.

B

The Rostonville Library which is built entirely of granite—a hard and very tough stone—is an example of durability. Granite is likely to remain strong and unaffected by environmental pollution. _____ Granite structures are stable and resistant to vibrations, so the Rostonville Library will likely be able to withstand an earthquake. The Rostonville Library is also durable in terms of sustainability, because it uses solar energy for heating, and a rooftop garden provides insulation that keeps the building cool in hot weather.

C

Designed to provide free access for members of the community to a variety of print and digital information, the Rostonville Library is also an example of Vitruvius's principle of functionality. The Rostonville Library conveys a feeling of openness and accessibility. _____ Furthermore, the entire library is on one level, and it has an open design—there are no interior walls or dividers. In addition, large windows let in plenty of natural light, so it's easy to see and get to each department within the library.

D

Finally, the Rostonville Library is beautiful. Aesthetically pleasing details make it attractive, both inside and out. The large windows are framed in copper. _____ Growth from the rooftop garden, that cascades down the sides of the building, adds to the aesthetics of the building. It softens the lines of the structure and helps it to blend into its natural surroundings. The library was built on the edge of the city park, which was designed using only native plants.

E

Durability, functionality, and beauty make the Rostonville Library a great structure. Architects and designers who follow Vitruvius's principles help to make urban environments more pleasant places to live. Structures that exemplify these criteria provide peace of mind as well as beauty for the people who use them.

D Now use the questions below to revise your essay.

REVISED DRAFT

- ☐ Does your introduction provide relevant background information on the topic?
- ☐ Does your thesis state the main points of the essay?
- ☐ Do your body paragraphs include enough details to fully explain your ideas?
- ☐ Did you use restrictive and nonrestrictive adjective clauses correctly?
- ☐ Do all your sentences relate to the main idea?
- ☐ Does your concluding paragraph have a summary statement and a final thought?

EDITING PRACTICE

Read the information below. Then find and correct one mistake with nonrestrictive adjective clauses in each of the sentences (1–4).

When using nonrestrictive adjective clauses, remember to:

• use one comma before a nonrestrictive adjective clause that appears at the end of a sentence. Use two commas, one before and one after, when the nonrestrictive adjective clause appears in the middle of a sentence.

• use *which* (not *that*) for objects in nonrestrictive adjective clauses.

1. This image is an excellent example of composition which is the way objects are arranged in a photograph.

2. That photograph, that I like best of all, is Berenice Abbott's *Pennsylvania Station*.

3. Another important element is light, that illuminates the objects in a photograph.

4. Moment which captures time in a photograph helps to tell the image's story.

FINAL DRAFT **E** Follow the steps to write a final draft.

1. Check your revised draft for mistakes with adjective clauses.

2. Now use the checklist on page 248 to write a final draft. Make any other necessary changes

UNIT REVIEW

Answer the following questions.

1. What are three important elements of a good photograph?

_____

_____

2. What do you think is the most important element in a beautiful photograph?

_____

_____

3. What is the purpose of a nonrestrictive clause?

_____

_____

4. Do you remember the meanings of these words? Check (✓) the ones you know. Look back at the unit and review the ones you don't know.

☐ balance
☐ composition
☐ context AWL
☐ crucial AWL
☐ depression AWL
☐ ethics AWL
☐ expose to AWL
☐ geometric

☐ imperfect
☐ insight AWL
☐ notion AWL
☐ principle AWL
☐ proportion AWL
☐ pursue AWL
☐ violate AWL

RETHINKING BUSINESS 4

A "break out space" designed to encourage creativity among staff at Google's London office

THINK AND DISCUSS

1 What are the most successful businesses in your country?

2 What made those businesses successful? How are those businesses different to other companies?

71

A Look at the information on these pages and answer the questions.

1. Which country exports the most clothing? In which country do people spend the most on clothing?

2. Which of the facts below is most interesting? Why?

B Match the correct form of the words in blue to their definitions.

_____ (n) clothing

_____ (n) the sale of goods to the public

_____ (n) the financial gain a company or a person makes

_____ (n) a person or business that you are competing with

FASHION FACTS

Fashion is big business. The global apparel market is valued at around 2.4 trillion dollars and accounts for 2 percent of the world's Gross Domestic Product (GDP).

These are the three largest fashion companies in the world—each making billions of dollars of profits each year. Nike's closest rival in the sportswear business, Adidas, is ranked number 5, after the fashion retail outlet, TJ Maxx.

1 Dior
$43.6 billion in sales

2 Nike
$33.8 billion in sales

3 Inditex
$25.7 billion in sales

There are **24.8 million** people in the world working to make clothes. China, the world's largest exporter of cloth and clothing, has over 10 million people working in the industry. They can make over 40 billion items of clothing in a year.

On average, Australians spend the most money on clothing.

Total Yearly Spending on Apparel Per Capita* (in US$) (2015):

1. Australia	$1,050
2. Canada	$831
3. Japan	$814
4. United States	$686
5. The European Union	$663
6. Brazil	$273
7. Russia	$272
8. China	$109

*Per capita means per person in the country.

The fashion industry has a huge impact on the environment. For example, it takes **2,700** liters of water to make just one cotton shirt. That's enough water for a person to drink for two and a half years!

A model showcases the hanbok, a form of traditional Korean dress. The traditional outfit has seen a growth in popularity in recent years. Hanbok purchases by women in South Korea increased by 80 percent between 2013 and 2016.

Reading

PREPARING TO READ

BUILDING
VOCABULARY

A The words in **blue** below are used in the reading passage. Match the correct form of each word to its definition.

Nearly 80 years ago, a woman named Yoon Dokjeong began selling hand-pressed camellia oil as a hair treatment in her home of Kaesong, in what is now North Korea. As a boy, her son Suh Sunghwan worked alongside his mother as she taught him how to make skincare products from natural materials. In 1945, Suh Sunghwan **founded** the South Korean cosmetics company AmorePacific. The company has its **headquarters** in Seoul, South Korea, and owns 30 cosmetic **brands**, including Laneige and Annick Goutal. Today, Yoon Dokjeong's grandson, Suh Kyungbae, is the company's CEO (chief **executive** officer). A great success in a very **competitive** industry, AmorePacific earned a profit of 811.5 billion won (US$707.2 million) in 2016.

1. _____ (adj) describing a situation or activity in which people or companies are trying to be more successful than others

2. _____ (v) to start a company, institution, or other organization

3. _____ (n) a senior-level employee who is responsible for making important decisions for the company

4. _____ (n) a product (or group of products) with its own name

5. _____ (n) an organization or company's main offices or center of control

▶ **Suh Kyungbae speaks to the media during AmorePacific's 70th anniversary conference.**

B Complete each sentence with the correct form of a word or phrase in the box. Use a dictionary to help you.

competitor	marketing	merchandise
outsource	shortage	supply chain

1. _____ is the activity of promoting and advertising goods or services in order to encourage people to buy them.

2. A company's _____ is someone who is trying to sell similar goods or services to the same people.

3. When a company _____ something, it pays workers from outside the company to do the work or supply the things it needs or sells.

4. If there is a _____ of something, there is not enough of it.

5. The things or goods a person or company sells is their _____.

6. A(n) _____ is the process involved in moving a product from supplier to customer.

C Discuss these questions with a partner.

1. What famous clothing **brands** do you know? Make a list below.

_____

_____

2. What do you know about the companies that make your favorite clothing brands? When were they **founded**? Where are their **headquarters**?

D Look back at your list of clothing brands in **C**. What makes each brand special? Note your ideas below. Then discuss with a partner.

_____

_____

E Skim the reading passage. What is it mainly about? Circle the correct option. Then read the passage to check your answers.

a. It describes the challenges of starting a clothing company.

b. It compares one company with other similar companies.

c. It explains how clothing is designed and manufactured.

CHANGING FASHION

by Mike W. Peng

> In the world of fast fashion, rather than only releasing a few new collections each year, companies like Zara sell a never-ending cycle of trend-led clothing, all year round.

A

Zara is now one of the world's hottest fashion chains. **Founded** in 1975, its parent company,[1] Inditex, has become a leading global **apparel** retailer. Since its initial public offering (IPO)[2] in 2001, Inditex, which owns eight fashion **brands**, has doubled the number of its stores. It has quadrupled its sales to US$25.7 billion, and its **profits** have risen to over US$3 billion. Zara contributes two-thirds of Inditex's total sales. In this intensely **competitive** industry, the secret to Zara's success is that Zara excels in **supply chain** management. In fact, Zara succeeds by first breaking and then rewriting industry rules.

Industry rule number one: *The origins of a fashion house usually carry a certain cachet.*[3] This is why most European fashion houses have their **headquarters** in Paris or Milan. However,

B

Zara does not hail from Italy or France—it is from Spain. Even within Spain, Zara is not based in a cosmopolitan city like Barcelona or Madrid. Its headquarters are in Arteixo, a town of only 25,000 people in a remote corner of northwestern Spain. Yet Zara is active not only throughout Europe, but also in Asia and North America. Currently, it has more than 5,000 stores in 88 countries, and these stores can be found in some truly pricey locations: the Champs-Elysees in Paris, Fifth Avenue in New York, Galleria in Dallas, Ginza in Tokyo, Queen's Road Central in Hong Kong, and Huaihai Road in Shanghai.

[1]A **parent company** is a company that owns smaller businesses.
[2]When a company has an **initial public offering**, it sells its stock to the public for the very first time.
[3]If something has a certain **cachet**, it has a quality that makes people admire it.

Rule number two: *Avoid stock-outs* (running out of in-demand items). From Zara's point of view, stock-outs are a good thing, since occasional **shortages** contribute to a shopper's urge to "buy now." At Zara, items sell out fast, with new products arriving at **retail** outlets twice a week. "If you see something and don't buy it," said one shopper, "you can forget about coming back for it because it will be gone." By giving just a short window of opportunity to purchase a limited quantity of **merchandise**, Zara's customers are motivated to visit the stores more frequently. In London, shoppers visit the average store four times a year, but frequent Zara 17 times. There is a good reason to do so, too: Zara makes and offers shoppers about 20,000 different items per year, about triple what stores like Gap do. "At Gap, everything is the same;" said one Zara customer. "Buying from Zara, you'll never end up looking like someone else."

Rule number three: *Bombarding[4] shoppers with ads is a must.* Traditionally, stores like Gap and H&M spend an average of 4 percent of their total sales on ads. Zara takes a different approach. It devotes just 0.3 percent of its sales to ads. The high traffic[5] in its stores reduces the need for advertising in the media, so most of Zara's **marketing** serves as a reminder for shoppers to visit the stores.

Rule number four: *Outsource for cheaper production.* Stores like Gap and H&M do not own any production facilities. They pay other companies to make their products, sometimes in places far away from their headquarters. However, outsourcing production (mostly to Asia) requires a long lead time[6]—usually several months. In contrast, Zara once again deviated from the norm. By concentrating more than half of its production in-house—in Arteixo, Spain, and nearby, in Portugal and Morocco—Zara has

developed a super-responsive supply chain. This means it can design, produce, and deliver a new item of clothing to its stores in a mere 15 *days*, a pace that is unheard of in the industry. The best speed most of its **rivals** can achieve is two months. Also, outsourcing may not necessarily be "low cost." Errors in trend prediction can easily lead to unsold inventory,[7] forcing their retail stores to offer steep discounts. The industry average is to offer 40 percent discounts across all merchandise. In contrast, Zara's ability to design

[7]An **inventory** is a supply or stock of something—the number of items that a store has for sale.

[4]If you **bombard** someone with something, you make them face a great deal of it.
[5]When a place has **high traffic**, it is crowded and has many people coming and going.
[6]In the production process, the **lead time** is the period of time between the decision to make a product and the completion of actual production.

and make new clothes quickly means shorter lead times and an ever-changing inventory. So it sells more at full price, and—when it discounts—averages only 15 percent.

Rule number five: *Strive for efficiency through large batches.* By producing products in large quantities, as is the industry norm, companies can benefit from economies of scale.[8] Zara, however, intentionally deals in small batches. Because of

[8]**Economies of scale** refers to the proportionate savings in costs gained when the level of production increases.

the greater flexibility and speed this approach affords, Zara does not worry about missing the boat when it comes to trends. When new trends emerge, Zara can react quickly. Also, it runs its supply chain like clockwork with a fast but predictable rhythm: Every store places orders on Tuesday/Wednesday and Friday/Saturday. Trucks and cargo flights run on established schedules—like a bus service. From Spain, shipments reach most European stores in 24 hours, U.S. stores in 48 hours, and Asian stores in 72 hours. And it is not only store staff who know exactly when

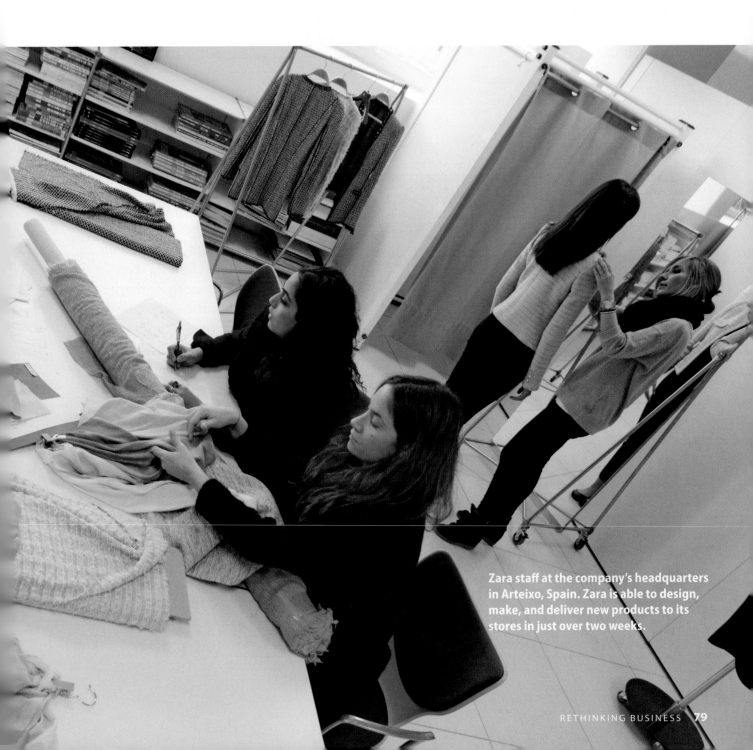

Zara staff at the company's headquarters in Arteixo, Spain. Zara is able to design, make, and deliver new products to its stores in just over two weeks.

shipments will arrive, but regular customers too. This motivates them to check out the new merchandise more frequently, especially on the shipment arrival days, known by Zara fans as "Z days."

Certainly, Zara has no shortage of **competitors**. But few have successfully copied its fast fashion and flexible business model. "I would love to organize our business like Inditex [Zara's parent]," noted an **executive** from Gap, "but I would have to knock my company down and rebuild it from scratch." This does not mean Gap and other rivals are not trying to copy Zara. The question is how long it takes for Zara's rivals to out-Zara Zara.

*Adapted from **Global Business** 4th Edition, by Mike W. Peng, © Cengage Learning 2015*

Mike W. Peng is the Jindal Chair of Global Business Strategy at the University of Texas at Dallas. A National Science Foundation (NSF) CAREER Award winner, Professor Peng is a fellow with the Academy of International Business and listed among Thomson Reuters' The World's Most Influential Scientific Minds.

ZARA: BIRTH OF A BRAND

In 1963, in the unremarkable seaside town of La Coruña, Spain, 27-year-old Amancio Ortega Gaona started a business making bathrobes. By 1975, Ortega had saved enough money from this business to open a clothing store in town. He named his store Zorba, after the movie *Zorba the Greek*. However, he soon learned that there was a bar in town called Zorba just a couple of blocks away. The bar owner thought that it might be confusing to have two businesses in town with the same name, so Ortega agreed to change the name of his store. The problem was that he had already made the letter molds for the store's sign. Rather than having new molds made, Ortega used some of the letters he already had molds for, and came up with a new name: Zara.

UNDERSTANDING THE READING

A Choose the statement that best summarizes the writer's main idea.

UNDERSTANDING
MAIN IDEAS

   a. Zara is successful because it follows established norms of the fashion industry.

   b. Zara has achieved success because it is run differently from other clothing companies.

   c. Zara owes its success to closely following the practices of other clothing companies.

B According to the passage, how does Zara operate its business? Check (✓) all that apply.

UNDERSTANDING
SUPPORTING IDEAS

   ☐ a. It manufactures small numbers of items at a time, so it can get them into stores quickly.

   ☐ b. It spends a lot of money on advertising.

   ☐ c. The company headquarters are based in a major city.

   ☐ d. Most Zara items are made in Spain or in nearby countries.

   ☐ e. It creates a certain cachet by charging high prices for clothing.

   ☐ f. It intentionally runs out of styles and replaces them with new ones.

> **CRITICAL THINKING** Some words are commonly grouped together to make **multiword units or phrases**. In these phrases, words often have different meanings than they do when they're used individually. It's important to learn these words as units and to use context to help you understand what they mean.

C Find and underline the following multiword phrases in the reading passage. Then circle the best meaning for each phrase.

CRITICAL THINKING:
UNDERSTANDING
MULTIWORD UNITS

1. Something that **serves as a reminder** _____.

   a. distracts people from doing that thing

   b. helps people remember to do that thing

2. Someone who has **deviated from the norm** has _____.

   a. followed well-established ways of doing things

   b. done something different from what was expected

3. If you **miss the boat**, you _____.

   a. do not understand a new idea correctly

   b. are too late to take advantage of an opportunity

4. If something operates **like clockwork**, it _____.

   a. works on a regular schedule

   b. has very complex working parts

5. If you rebuild something **from scratch**, you build it _____.

   a. again, from the beginning

   b. in its old building, with some changes

D Complete the missing bars in the charts using information from the reading passage.

1. **Inditex Sales:**
   2001 vs. Today

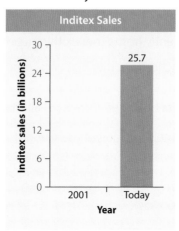

2. **Average Store Visits per Year:**
   Zara vs. Average London Stores

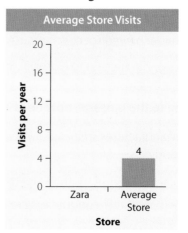

3. **No. of Items Made per Year:**
   Zara vs. Gap

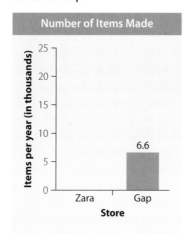

4. **Spending on Advertising:**
   Zara vs. Gap / H&M

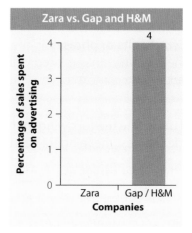

5. **Days from Design to in Store:**
   Zara vs. Competitors

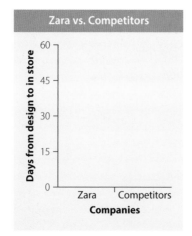

6. **Discounts on Unsold Inventory:**
   Zara vs. Industry Average

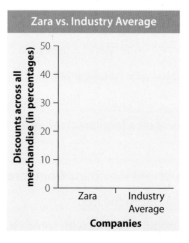

DEVELOPING READING SKILLS

> **READING SKILL** Understanding Sentences with Initial Phrases
>
> Writers often put prepositional, time, and verbal phrases at the beginnings of sentences, before the main clause. Writers use initial phrases to vary their sentence structure and to change the emphasis in a sentence.
>
> **Founded in 1975,** its parent company, Inditex, has become a leading global apparel retailer.
>
> **Since its initial public offering (IPO) in 2001,** Inditex, … has doubled the number of its stores.

A Look back at paragraphs C, D, E, and F in the reading passage. Find and underline all the initial phrases.

B Answer the questions. Use information from initial phrases you identified in **A.**

UNDERSTANDING SENTENCES WITH INITIAL PHRASES

1. Why are customers motivated to visit Zara stores more frequently than other stores?

   a. because items in Zara stores are only available for a relatively short time

   b. because Zara will regularly offer huge discounts on many of its products

2. How has Zara developed a super-responsive supply chain?

   a. by making most of its clothing in or near its headquarters

   b. by having factories in many different countries around the world

3. How do most fashion companies take advantage of economies of scale?

   a. by selling their items in huge stores

   b. by producing products in large batches

4. Why is Zara not worried about missing the boat when it comes to trends?

   a. because its designers are extremely good at predicting future fashion trends

   b. because it can keep up with trends by designing and making new products quickly

◀ **Boxes of ready-to-wear garments are prepared at Zara's headquarters in Arteixo, Spain.**

Italian fashion designer
Brunello Cucinelli

BEHIND THE BRAND

BEFORE VIEWING

DISCUSSION **A** What famous fashion designers do you know? What are they known for? Discuss with a partner.

_____

_____

LEARNING ABOUT THE TOPIC **B** Read the information. Then answer the questions.

Brunello Cucinelli is a luxury Italian fashion brand that sells high-end menswear and womenswear in countries around the world. The company—best known for its cashmere sweaters—had humble beginnings. Founder Brunello Cucinelli first started out dying cashmere in a small workshop. After some success, he founded the company in 1978, and since then, the brand has gone from strength to strength. Nowadays, Cucinelli is a highly influential figure in the fashion industry, and in the last ten years, the company has quadrupled in size.

1. What kinds of fashion products does the company Brunello Cucinelli make?

_____

2. What factors do you think make a fashion brand successful?

_____

_____

C The words in **bold** below are used in the video. Match the correct form of each word to its definition.

> Versace, Gucci, and Armani are three of the most famous **high-end** fashion brands.
>
> In many parts of the world, working conditions are improving thanks to **enlightened** business owners recognizing the importance of workers' rights.
>
> The rise of big businesses has led to fewer and fewer people being able to make a living as self-employed **artisans**.
>
> Calvin Klein founded his **eponymous** fashion brand in New York in 1968.

1. _____ (adj) named after a particular person

2. _____ (adj) expensive and luxurious

3. _____ (adj) having modern, well-informed opinions

4. _____ (n) someone who works with their hands in a skilled profession

WHILE VIEWING

A ▶ Watch the video. According to the video, which two of the following have contributed to fashion brand Brunello Cucinelli's success?

- ☐ a. its ethical employment practices
- ☐ b. its location in a traditional Italian village
- ☐ c. its investment in foreign talent
- ☐ d. its use of modern technology

B ▶ Watch the video again. Note answers to the questions below. Then discuss with a partner.

1. How does Brunello Cucinelli ensure that its staff don't work too much?

_____

_____

2. In what ways has founder Brunello Cucinelli helped the local village?

_____

_____

AFTER VIEWING

A What does Cucinelli mean when he says, "I don't think it's time wasted watching a bird in the sky when you're sewing a button"? Discuss with a partner.

B In what ways are Zara and Brunello Cucinelli similar? In what ways are they different? Note your ideas below. Then discuss with a partner.

_____

_____

Writing

EXPLORING WRITTEN ENGLISH

A The following words and phrases can be useful when writing a comparative essay. Some are used to show similarities, and some are used to show differences. Put each word in the correct category.

although	both	conversely	equally
have in common	however	in contrast (to)	in the same way (that)
instead (of)	likewise	on the contrary	on the other hand
similarly	the same is true for	whereas	unlike

Similarities	Differences

LANGUAGE FOR WRITING Using Sentences with Initial Phrases

You can use initial phrases (prepositional, time, and verbal phrases) to avoid short, choppy sentences. Using initial phrases is also a way to vary your sentence style and to show the relationship between ideas. Remember to use a comma to separate the initial phrase from the main clause.

To avoid short, choppy sentences:

Samsung first started business in 1938. It was originally a trading company.

Founded in 1938, *Samsung was originally a trading company.* (verbal phrase)

To vary sentence style and/or show the relationship between ideas:

Ortega changed his store's name to Zara when he discovered that the name Zorba was already being used.

When he discovered that the name Zorba was already being used, *Ortega changed his store's name to Zara.* (time phrase)

Sergey Brin developed a search engine that would become Google in a friend's garage.

In a friend's garage, *Sergey Brin developed a search engine that would become Google.* (prepositional phrase)

B Rewrite each sentence to include an initial phrase.

1. H&M only sold women's clothing when it opened for business in 1947.

   When _____

2. Karl-Johan Persson became H&M's CEO in 2009.

   _____

3. BRS distributed shoes for a Japanese shoe maker until the spring of 1971.

   _____

4. The company's name was changed to Nike when BRS's relationship with the Japanese shoe maker ended.

   _____

WRITING SKILL Organizing a Comparative Essay

There are two main ways to organize a comparative essay: the **block method** and the **point-by-point method**.

With the **block method**, you discuss all the points of comparison about one subject and then discuss those same points about the other subject. The outline looks like this:

Introduction + Thesis statement

Body paragraph 1: Subject A

       Point 1

       Point 2

       Point 3

Body paragraph 2: Subject B

       Point 1

       Point 2

       Point 3

Conclusion

With the **point-by-point method**, you discuss each subject in terms of the points of comparison you've chosen. If there are three points of comparison, the outline looks like this:

Introduction + Thesis statement

Body paragraph 1: Point 1

       Subject A

       Subject B

Body paragraph 2: Point 2

       Subject A

       Subject B

Body paragraph 3: Point 3

       Subject A

       Subject B

Conclusion

C Look at the notes for a comparative essay on two companies. Use the notes to fill in the outline for a block comparative essay.

Notes

	Apple	Samsung
Early years	founded in Silicon Valley, United States, 1976, as tech company by S. Jobs, S. Wozniak, R. Wayne	founded in Taegu, Korea, 1938, as trading company, by Lee Byung-Chul
Marketing	direct advertising, not much social media, famous for TV ads	relies heavily on social media, celebrity endorsements, sponsorship of global events
Product development	long time to create new products, e.g. iPad	faster than Apple to assess consumer interest/marketability

OUTLINE

Organization method: ___Block_____

Notes for introduction: _Apple and Samsung are both highly successful tech companies_

_____

Thesis statement: _____

_____

Body paragraph 1:

Topic sentence: _____

Details: _____

_____

_____

Body paragraph 2:

Topic sentence: _____

Details: _____

_____

_____

Notes for conclusion: _____

_____

_____

WRITING TASK

GOAL You are going to write a comparative essay on the following topic:

Compare two companies in the same industry. Consider aspects such as their history, location, product types, and business practices.

BRAINSTORMING

A Choose an industry that you are interested in and two companies to compare. Complete the Venn diagram with at least three similarities and/or differences that you know about between the two companies. Research additional information.

Industry: _____

Company 1: _____   **Company 2:** _____

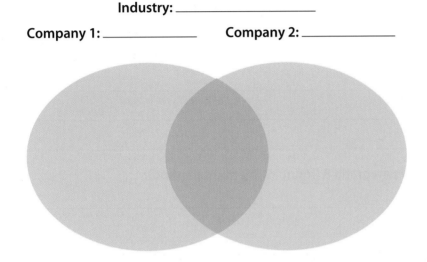

PLANNING

B Follow the steps to make notes for your essay.

Step 1 Look at your brainstorming notes. Identify the three points of comparison that you want to write about. Summarize them in the thesis statement in the outline. Note some ideas for an introduction.

Step 2 Choose an organization method for your essay. Depending on your organizational method, complete the outline.

Step 3 Write a topic sentence for each body paragraph and note some examples or details that illustrate your comparison.

Step 4 Note some ideas for a conclusion.

OUTLINE

Organization method (block or point-by-point): _____

Notes for introduction: _____

_____

Thesis statement: _____

_____

Body paragraph 1:

Topic sentence: _____

_____

Details: _____

_____

_____

Body paragraph 2:

Topic sentence: _____

_____

Details: _____

_____

_____

Body paragraph 3 (for point-by-point method):

Topic sentence: _____

_____

Details: _____

_____

_____

Notes for conclusion: _____

_____

FIRST DRAFT **C** Use the information in your outline to write a first draft of your essay.

REVISING PRACTICE

The draft on the opposite page is a model of the essay you are writing. Follow the steps to create a better second draft.

1. Add the sentences or phrases (a–c) in the correct spaces.

   a. In contrast to Apple's direct marketing strategies,
   b. Apple Inc. is one of the largest information technology companies in the world.
   c. For example, its 2014 "Your Verse" campaign highlighted different ways people use their iPads (Beltrone, 2014).

2. Now fix the following problems (a–c) with the essay.

   a. Fix a problem with an initial phrase in paragraph B.
   b. Fix a problem with an initial phrase in paragraph C.
   c. Fix a problem with a comparison word in paragraph C.

A

From phones to tablets to TVs, Apple and Samsung products are household names around the world. In fact, both companies seem to dominate the mobile phone industry. However, while the two companies have certain features in common, they differ in terms of history, marketing styles, and the way they develop their products.

B

_____ Founded in 1976, in the heart of Silicon Valley Apple originally focused on the development and marketing of personal computers. Its founders were Steve Jobs, Steve Wozniak, and Ronald Wayne, and its early products included the Apple I, the Lisa, and the Macintosh. Today, Apple is known around the world for its well-designed phones, tablets, and other tech devices. In terms of marketing, Apple relies primarily on direct advertising and does not use social media to promote its products as much as other tech companies do. In fact, Apple is famous for its distinctive television ads. _____ Regarding product development and release, Apple usually takes quite a long time to create new products. For example, the company spent eight years developing the iPad. This reflects a key aspect of Apple's corporate culture: a determination to never release anything to the market unless it's perfect (Kaslikowski, 2013).

C

While Samsung, like Apple, is a technology company today, Samsung started out as a trading company in Taegu, Korea. Founded, in 1938 by Lee Byung-Chul, Samsung began as a grocery store, "trading and exporting goods produced in and around the city, like dried Korean fish and vegetables, as well as its own noodles" (Burris, 2017). Today, as a large conglomerate owning multiple companies, Samsung is one of the largest businesses in Korea. _____ Samsung relies heavily on social media as an avenue for advertising. The company also promotes its product with celebrity endorsements; participation in, and sponsorship of, global events; and discounts. Finally, likewise Apple spends a long time on product development, Samsung releases products in less time with the goal of assessing consumer interest and marketability. When a product is judged to be popular with consumers, then it is refined and improved.

D

Although both Apple and Samsung are leaders in the mobile phone market, their histories and strategies are distinctive. Over the years, the competitive nature of the technology industry has challenged the two companies to make each new phone more innovative than the last. Due to this, and the fact that Apple and Samsung are in intense competition with each other, it is likely the two companies will continue to create groundbreaking products far into the future.

References

Beltrone, Gabriel. (2014, Aug. 12). Apple's powerful "your verse" campaign rolls on, from Beijing and through Detroit. AdWeek. Retrieved from http://www.adweek.com/creativity/apples-powerful-your-verse-campaign-rolls-beijing-and-through-detroit-159442/.

Burris, Matthew. (2017, Sept. 7). The History of Samsung (1938-Present): Who Founded Samsung, When Samsung Was Created, and Other Facts. Lifewire. Retrieved from https://www.lifewire.com/history-of-samsung-818809.

Kaslikowski, Adam. (2013, Sept. 5). The difference between Samsung and Apple. Lucky Robot. Retrieved from http://luckyrobot.com/difference-between-samsung-and-apple/.

D Now use the questions below to revise your essay.

☐ Does your introduction have an interesting hook?

☐ Does your thesis state the main points of the essay?

☐ Did you use the block method or the point-by-point method to organize your essay?

☐ Do your body paragraphs include enough details to fully explain your ideas?

☐ Did you use initial phrases correctly?

☐ Does your concluding paragraph have a summary statement and a final thought?

EDITING PRACTICE

Read the information in the box. Then find and correct one mistake with initial phrases in each sentence (1–3).

In sentences with initial phrases, remember to:
• use a comma to separate the initial phrase from the main clause
• use a prepositional, time, or verbal phrase as the initial phase

1. In 1975 Steve Wozniak, and Steve Jobs built the first Apple computer.

2. It was founded in 1949, Adidas is now one of the world's leading sports brands.

3. Offering innovative tech products Samsung is one of the most successful businesses in Korea.

FINAL DRAFT **E** Follow the steps to write a final draft.

1. Check your revised draft for mistakes with referring to sources.

2. Now use the checklist on page 248 to write a final draft. Make any other necessary changes.

UNIT REVIEW

Answer the following questions.

1. What are two ways in which Zara differs from other clothing companies?

_____

_____

2. What are two ways in which Brunello Cucinelli is different from Zara?

_____

_____

3. What are two ways to organize a comparative essay?

_____

_____

4. Do you remember the meanings of these words? Check (✔) the ones you know. Look back at the unit and review the ones you don't know.

☐ apparel   ☐ merchandise

☐ brand   ☐ outsource

☐ competitive ☐ profit

☐ competitor ☐ retail

☐ executive   ☐ rival

☐ found AWL   ☐ shortage

☐ headquarters ☐ supply chain

☐ marketing

WORKING TOGETHER 5

A four-man bobsleigh team prepares for its first run at the 2017 BMW IBSF World Cup in Innsbruck, Austria.

ACADEMIC SKILLS

READING	Understanding complex sentences
WRITING	Writing a summary essay
GRAMMAR	Avoiding plagiarism (I) — Paraphrasing
CRITICAL THINKING	Evaluating sources

THINK AND DISCUSS

1 In what situations do people work together in groups to make decisions or solve problems?
2 What are some advantages of working together in large groups? What are some of the disadvantages?

A Look at the information on these pages and answer the questions.

1. How is the photo an example of collaboration?
2. In what ways did primitive people collaborate?
3. What are some modern examples of collaboration? What purposes do they serve?

B Match the correct form of the words in blue to their definitions.

_____ (v) to succeed in doing something

_____ (adv) as a group

_____ (adj) difficult to understand; not simple

COLLABORATION

People collaborate when they work together to **accomplish** a task. Collaboration among early humans helped to ensure their survival. For example, early humans used teamwork in order to find food and raise children. In the modern world, collaboration is a key feature in organizational settings such as businesses—most organizational behavior experts agree, for example, that collaboration increases productivity. When people work together, they can use each other's knowledge to advance new ideas and solve **complex** problems.

In recent years, collaboration has been greatly enhanced by the Internet. In the past, people had to be in the same place in order to work together. Today, online collaboration allows people to accomplish a range of tasks **collectively** at any time and from any location. Crowdsourcing, which uses a network of a large number of people to help solve a problem, is increasing our scientific knowledge. Data collected from a crowdsourcing website called Cerberus, for example, is helping astronomers analyze satellite images of Mars.

What makes humans want to collaborate? James K. Rilling, an anthropologist at Emory University, looked at brain activity while participants were engaged in cooperative activities. His study showed that the desire to cooperate with others may be innate in humans. Researchers are also looking into ways to enhance human collaboration. Studies of the ways in which animal and insect groups—such as ants—collaborate may help us figure out ways to work together even more efficiently.

Contestants work together to construct a human tower during the 26th Tarragona Competition in Tarragona, Spain.

Reading

PREPARING TO READ

A The words in **blue** below are used in the reading passage. Match the correct word to its definition.

Insects may help us improve the way we deal with dangerous situations. Scientists around the world are studying insect behavior to create tiny robots that have many of the same **capabilities** as insects. Insects, for example, can fly in and land **precisely** on a tiny surface, and then flap their wings to fly off with amazing speed. One application for these tiny insectlike machines is in **defense**—robots will be able to scout battlefields and record images as they hover over dangerous areas. Engineers are also building ornithopters—aircraft that get all of their thrust and most of their lift from flapping wings. The flight mechanism of an ornithopter is essentially a **simulation** of the way that an insect flaps its wings to take off and fly. These **emergent** technologies offer several advantages. One benefit is that operators can **manipulate** the devices from a distance. As a result, they can stay out of harm's way while they perform dangerous missions in **unpredictable** environments, such as war zones.

1. _____ (n) action taken to protect against attack; also, the organization of a country's armies and weapons

2. _____ (v) to control, manage, or use carefully

3. _____ (n) a model; imitation of behaviors or processes

4. _____ (n) skills or qualities

5. _____ (adj) not able to be known in advance

6. _____ (adj) coming into existence

7. _____ (adv) accurately and exactly

B Complete the definitions with the words in the box. Use a dictionary to help you.

complementary	coordinate	declare	relevant	realistically

1. If people _____ something, they formally announce it.

2. Something that is _____ to a situation is important or significant.

3. To _____ with others is to work together efficiently.

4. When people show things _____, they show them in a way that is accurate and true to life.

5. _____ things are different from each other, but they make a good combination.

C Note answers to the questions below. Then discuss with a partner.

USING VOCABULARY

1. What are some **capabilities** of groups versus individuals?

   _____

   _____

2. Think of a group that you belong to. Are the skills of the group members **complementary**? Give examples.

   _____

   _____

3. Do you like to **coordinate** with others on projects? Why or why not?

   _____

   _____

D Note answers to the questions below. Then discuss in a small group.

BRAINSTORMING

1. What are some examples of group behavior among animals?

   _____

   _____

2. For what kinds of jobs is collaboration very important?

   _____

   _____

E Look at the photos and captions in the reading passage. Read the first and last paragraphs (A and V). Note answers to the questions below. Then discuss with a partner. Check your predictions as you read the rest of the passage.

PREVIEWING

1. What animals might the passage discuss?

   _____

   _____

2. What aspects of their behavior might the passage discuss?

   _____

   _____

3. What human activities or inventions might the passage discuss?

   _____

   _____

4. What do you think is the main purpose of the article?

   _____

   _____

THE SMART SWARM

by Peter Miller

Monarch butterflies in flight in Michoacan, Mexico

> The study of swarms is providing insights that can help humans manage complex systems, from online search engines to military robots.

🎧 1.5

How do the simple actions of individuals add up to the **complex** behavior of a group? How do hundreds of honeybees make a critical decision about their hive if many of them disagree? What enables a school of herring to **coordinate** its movements so **precisely** it can change direction in a flash—like a single, silvery organism? The answer has to do with a remarkable phenomenon I call *the smart swarm.*

A smart swarm is a group of individuals who respond to one another and to their environment in ways that give them the power, as a group, to cope with uncertainty, complexity, and change. Take birds, for example. There's a small park near the White House in Washington, D.C., where I like to watch flocks of pigeons swirl over the traffic and trees. Sooner or later, the birds come to rest on ledges of buildings surrounding the park. Then something disrupts them, and they're off again in synchronized flight.

The birds don't have a leader. No pigeon is telling the others what to do. Instead, they're each paying close attention to the pigeons next to them, each bird following simple rules as they wheel across the sky. These rules add up to a kind of swarm intelligence—one that has to do with precisely coordinating movement.

Craig Reynolds, a computer graphics researcher, was curious about what these rules might be. So, in 1986, he created a deceptively simple steering program called boids. In this simulation, generic birdlike objects, or boids, were each given three instructions: (1) avoid crowding nearby boids, (2) fly in the average direction of nearby boids, and (3) stay close to nearby boids. The result, when set in motion on a computer screen, was a convincing **simulation** of flocking,[1] including lifelike and **unpredictable** movements.

At the time, Reynolds was looking for ways to depict animals **realistically** in TV shows and movies. (*Batman Returns* in 1992 was the first movie to use his approach, portraying a swarm of bats and an army of penguins.) Today he works at Sony doing research for games, such as an algorithm[2] that simulates in real time as many as 15,000 interacting birds, fish, or people.

By demonstrating the power of self-organizing models to mimic swarm behavior, Reynolds was also blazing the trail for robotics engineers. A team of robots that could coordinate its actions like a flock of birds could offer significant advantages over a solitary robot. Spread out over a large area, a group could function as a powerful mobile sensor net, gathering information about what's out there. If the group encountered something unexpected, it could adjust and respond quickly, even if the robots in the group

---

[1] When animals **flock**, they congregate and do things as a large group.
[2] An **algorithm** is a process to be followed in performing a calculation, especially by a computer.

Safety in numbers: A school of sardines acts as a single entity to defend against attack by an Atlantic sailfish.

weren't very sophisticated—just as ants are able to come up with various options by trial and error. If one member of the group were to break down, others could take its place. And, most important, control of the group could be decentralized, not dependent on a leader.

"In biology, if you look at groups with large numbers, there are very few examples where you have a central agent," says Vijay Kumar, a professor of mechanical engineering at the University of Pennsylvania. "Everything is very distributed: They don't all talk to each other. They act on local information. And they're all anonymous. I don't care who moves the chair, as long as somebody moves the chair. To go from one robot to multiple robots, you need all three of those ideas."

In the near future, Kumar hopes to put a networked team of robotic vehicles in the field. One purpose might be as first responders. "Let's say there's a 911 call," he says. "The fire alarm goes off. You don't want humans to respond. You want machines to respond, to tell you what's happening. Before you send firemen into a burning building, why not send in a group of robots?"

Taking this idea one step further, computer scientist Marco Dorigo's group in Brussels is leading a European effort to create a "swarmanoid," a group of cooperating robots with complementary abilities: "foot-bots" to transport things on the ground, "hand-bots" to climb walls and manipulate objects, and "eye-bots" to fly around, providing information to the other units.

The military is eager to acquire similar capabilities. On January 20, 2004, researchers released a swarm of 66 pint-size robots into an empty office building at Fort A. P. Hill, a training center near Fredericksburg, Virginia. The mission: Find targets hidden in the building.

Zipping down the main hallway, the foot-long (30 cm) red robots pivoted this way and that on their three wheels, resembling a group of large insects. Eight sonars[3] on each unit helped them avoid collisions with walls and other robots. As they spread out, entering one room after another, each robot searched for objects of interest with a small camera. When one robot encountered another, it used wireless network gear to exchange information. ("Hey, I've already explored that part of the building. Look somewhere else.")

In the back of one room, a robot spotted something suspicious: a pink ball in an open closet (the swarm had been trained to look for anything pink). The robot froze, sending an image to its human supervisor. Soon, several more robots arrived to form a perimeter around the pink intruder. Within half an hour, the mission had been accomplished—all six of the hidden objects had been found. The research team conducting the experiment declared the run a success. Then they started a new test.

[3]**Sonar** is equipment that can detect the position of objects using sound waves.

The demonstration was part of the Centibots project, an investigation to see if as many as a hundred robots could collaborate on a mission. If they could, teams of robots might someday be sent into a hostile village to flush out terrorists or locate prisoners; into an earthquake-damaged building to find victims; onto chemical-spill sites to examine hazardous waste; or along borders to watch for intruders. Military agencies such as DARPA (**Defense** Advanced Research Projects Agency) have funded a number of robotics programs using collaborative flocks of helicopters and fixed-wing aircraft, schools of torpedo-shaped underwater gliders, and herds of unmanned ground vehicles. But, at the time, this was the largest swarm of robots ever tested.

"When we started Centibots, we were all thinking, this is a crazy idea, it's impossible to do," says Régis Vincent, a researcher at SRI International in Menlo Park, California. "Now we're looking to see if we can do it with a thousand robots."

Swarm-bots work together using swarm theory.

In nature, of course, animals travel in even larger numbers. That's because, as members of a big group, whether it's a flock, school, or herd, individuals increase their chances of detecting predators, finding food, locating a mate, or following a migration route. For these animals, coordinating their movements with one another can be a matter of life or death.

"It's much harder for a predator to avoid being spotted by a thousand fish than it is to avoid being spotted by one," says Daniel Grünbaum, a biologist at the University of Washington. "News that a predator is approaching spreads quickly through a school because fish sense from their neighbors that something's going on."

When a predator strikes a school of fish, the group is capable of scattering in patterns that make it almost impossible to track any individual. It might explode in a flash, create a kind of moving bubble around the predator, or fracture into multiple blobs,[4] before coming back together and swimming away.

That's the wonderful appeal of swarm intelligence. Whether we're talking about ants, bees, pigeons, or caribou, the ingredients of smart group behavior—decentralized control, response to local cues, simple rules of thumb—add up to a shrewd strategy to cope with complexity.

[4]A **blob** is an indistinct or a shapeless form or object.

A huge herd of wildebeest surge across the flooded Mara River in Serengeti National Park, Tanzania.

"We don't even know yet what else we can do with this," says Eric Bonabeau, a complexity theorist and the chief scientist at Icosystem Corporation in Cambridge, Massachusetts. "We're not used to solving decentralized problems in a decentralized way. We can't control an emergent phenomenon like traffic by putting stop signs and lights everywhere. But the idea of shaping traffic as a self-organizing system, that's very exciting."

The Internet is already using a form of swarm intelligence. Consider the way Google uses group smarts to find what you're looking for. When you type in a search query, Google surveys billions of Web pages on its index servers[5] to identify the most relevant ones. It then ranks them by the number of pages that link to them, counting links as votes (the most popular sites get weighted[6] votes since they're more likely to be reliable). The pages that receive the most votes are listed first in the search results. In this way, Google says, it "uses the collective intelligence of the Web to determine a page's importance."

Wikipedia, a free collaborative encyclopedia, has also proved to be a big success, with millions of articles in more than 200 languages about everything under the sun, each of which can be contributed by anyone or edited by anyone. "It's now possible for huge numbers of people to think together in ways we never imagined a few decades ago," says Thomas Malone of MIT's new Center for Collective Intelligence. "No single person knows everything that's needed to deal with problems we face as a society, such as health care or climate change, but collectively we know far more than we've been able to tap so far."

Such thoughts underline an important truth about collective intelligence: Crowds tend to be wise only if individual members act responsibly and make their own decisions. A group won't be smart if its members imitate one another, slavishly follow fads, or wait for someone to tell them what to do. When a group is being intelligent, whether it's made up of ants or attorneys, it relies on its members to do their own part. For those of us who sometimes wonder if it's really worth recycling that extra bottle to lighten our impact on the planet, the bottom line is that our actions matter, even if we don't see how.

[5]A server is a part of a computer network that does a particular task such as maintaining an index of files.
[6]If something is weighted, it is given more value according to how important it is.

Adapted from "Swarm Theory," by Peter Miller: National Geographic Magazine July 2007

Peter Miller has worked as a reporter for *Life* magazine and as a senior editor at *National Geographic*. He is the author of the best-selling book *The Smart Swarm: How to Work Efficiently, Communicate Effectively, and Make Better Decisions Using the Secrets of Flocks, Schools, and Colonies.*

UNDERSTANDING THE READING

UNDERSTANDING
MAIN IDEAS

A Note answers to the questions below. Write the paragraph letter(s) in which you find the answers.

1. What is a "smart swarm"? Explain it in your own words.

_____

_____ Paragraph _____

2. How does being part of a large group help animals?

_____

_____ Paragraph _____

3. What are the three key aspects of swarm intelligence?

_____

_____ Paragraph _____

4. How are search engines and online encyclopedias examples of collaboration?

_____

_____ Paragraph _____

UNDERSTANDING
PURPOSE

B Match each section of the reading to its main purpose. Write the paragraph letters.

B–C	D–N	O–Q	R	T–U	V

1. _____ to give examples of human activities and organizations that use swarm intelligence

2. _____ to summarize the three key ingredients of swarm intelligence

3. _____ to connect the topic with our everyday decisions and actions

4. _____ to show the purpose of swarm behavior for animals

5. _____ to give an example of swarm intelligence that most people are familiar with

6. _____ to describe technology applications that mimic swarm behavior

CRITICAL THINKING:
GUESSING MEANING
FROM CONTEXT

C Find and underline the following expressions in the reading passage. Use the context to match each expression with its definition.

1. _____ **add up to** (paragraph A)
2. _____ **set in motion** (paragraph D)
3. _____ **blazing the trail** (paragraph F)
4. _____ **by trial and error** (paragraph F)
5. _____ **flush out** (paragraph M)
6. _____ **a matter of life or death** (paragraph O)
7. _____ **the bottom line** (paragraph V)

a. to force people or animals to leave a place where they are hiding

b. the essential idea

c. to start; to initiate an action

d. to equal

e. something extremely important

f. doing something for the first time as an example for others

g. trying out different methods

D Complete the concept map with information from paragraphs B–N.

Swarm Intelligence

Example in the Animal World

- Flocks of ¹_____ are an example of swarm intelligence.

- **Characteristics:**
  (1) There's no ²_____.
  (2) They watch and follow
  ³_____.

Human Applications

Entertainment

- Used to create rules for computer graphics e.g., boids.

- **Rules:** (1) avoid crowding, (2) ⁴_____,
  (3) ⁵_____

Robot Teams

- **Advantages:** Robot teams respond more effectively than individual robots. If one breaks down, another can ⁶_____.

- **Rules:** Everything is distributed; they use ⁷_____; they're anonymous.

- **Examples:** ⁸_____ for moving things; ⁹_____ to climb walls and manipulate things; ¹⁰_____ to fly around and collect ¹¹_____.

- **Military uses:** Centibots could locate terrorists or ¹²_____; help people in disasters, such as ¹³_____; find and analyze dangerous ¹⁴_____ after a chemical spill.

CRITICAL THINKING   Writers often quote experts to support their main ideas. It's important to **evaluate** the source of each quote. When you read a quote, ask yourself: What are the credentials of the person being quoted? What is his or her background or affiliation? How is his or her experience or expertise relevant to the topic? Then ask yourself how the quotes support the writer's main ideas.

E   Find the following quotes in the reading. Note the paragraph where you find each one.

1. _____ "In biology, … you need all three of those ideas."

2. _____ "It's much harder for a predator … to avoid being spotted by one ….

   News that a predator is approaching spreads quickly … that something's going on."

3. _____ "It's now possible … in ways we never imagined a few decades ago ….

   No single person … we know far more than we've been able to tap so far."

Now discuss answers to the questions below with a partner.

1. What are the credentials of the people being quoted? How is their experience or expertise relevant to the topic?

2. What main ideas do the quotes support? Match each quote (1–3) with one of the following ideas.

   a. _____ Swarm behavior is a survival strategy.

   b. _____ Modern technology has facilitated swarm intelligence among humans.

   c. _____ Decentralization is a key aspect of swarm intelligence.

F   Look again at paragraph V. Note answers to the questions below. Then discuss with a partner.

1. According to the author, for crowd intelligence to work, how should the individuals behave?

   _____

   _____

2. What example of an everyday activity does the author give to illustrate this point?

   _____

   _____

3. What "smart swarms" are you a part of? Make a list.

   _____

   _____

DEVELOPING READING SKILLS

> **READING SKILL** Understanding Complex Sentences
>
> It's important for overall reading comprehension to be able to understand complex sentences. One way to do this is to break down complex sentences into smaller parts. Follow these steps:
>
> 1. Identify the main clause and any dependent clauses in the sentence.
>
>   **main clause**   **dependent clause**   **main clause**
>
>   A team of robots that could coordinate its actions like a flock of birds could offer significant advantages over a solitary robot.
>
> 2. Identify the subject, verb, and object in the main clause.
>
>   **subject**   **verb**   **object**
>
>   A team of robots … could offer significant advantages over a solitary robot.
>
> 3. Look back at the dependent clauses for any extra information to help you understand the full sentence.

A Use the steps above to break down the following complex sentences. Then answer the questions.

UNDERSTANDING COMPLEX SENTENCES

1. Taking this idea one step further, computer scientist Marco Dorigo's group in Brussels is leading a European effort to create a "swarmanoid," a group of cooperating robots with complementary abilities.

   a. What is Dorigo's group doing? _____

   b. What is a swarmanoid? _____

2. The result, when set in motion on a computer screen, was a convincing simulation of flocking, including lifelike and unpredictable movements.

   a. What was the result? _____

   b. What did the simulation include? _____

3. Zipping down the main hallway, the foot-long (30 cm) red robots pivoted this way and that on their three wheels, resembling a group of large insects.

   a. What was zipping down the main hallway? _____

   b. What did they look like? _____

B Scan paragraphs K, M, U, and V to find more examples of complex sentences. When you find them, underline the subjects and circle the main verbs.

APPLYING

Video

Fire ants form a floating raft on the surface of water.

ANT TEAMWORK

BEFORE VIEWING

DISCUSSION

A What types of group behavior have you seen ants display? Discuss with a partner.

_____

_____

LEARNING ABOUT
THE TOPIC

B Read the information. Then answer the questions.

Ants are known to be amazing collaborators—they work together to build homes, find food, and fight off their enemies. But perhaps one of the most astounding examples of ant teamwork is the ingenious way that fire ants are able to cope with flooding. If their home is flooded, fire ants will join themselves together, gripping tight with their jaws and legs, to form a pizza-like shape that can float on water like a raft. Some rafts can last up to three weeks, and it is thought that some of the bigger structures may have more than 100,000 ants. But if you see one, stay well clear. Fire ants have a painful sting and are thought to be even more aggressive than usual when in a raft formation.

1. Why do fire ants create rafts? How do they do it?

_____

2. How is this behavior an example of swarm intelligence?

_____

C Read these extracts from the video. Match the correct form of each **bold** word to its definition.

VOCABULARY IN CONTEXT

> "By identifying individuals, Nigel can tell who collects information, how they communicate it, and how a **consensus** is reached."
>
> "The ants begin **inspecting** their two options. Every time an individual enters or exits the potential nests, a laser beam records its passing."
>
> "They do a very special form of **recruitment** called tandem running. That's when one ant literally leads just a single other nest mate."

1. _____ (n) the process of getting individuals to join an organization, a group, or an activity

2. _____ (n) an agreement made by all members of a group

3. _____ (v) to look carefully at something to make a judgment about it

WHILE VIEWING

A ▶ Watch the video. Complete the sentences below.

UNDERSTANDING MAIN IDEAS

a. The purpose of the experiment is to _____.

b. In the experiment, the ants need to _____.

c. It takes the ants around _____ to make a successful choice.

B ▶ Watch the video again. Note answers to the question below.

UNDERSTANDING A PROCESS

1. Why were microchips attached to the ants?

_____

2. How does an individual ant report its findings?

_____

3. What is "tandem running"?

_____

AFTER VIEWING

A Dr. Franks says that "tandem-running qualifies as teaching." How do you think scientists decide if an action in the animal world qualifies as teaching? Discuss your ideas with a partner.

REACTING TO THE VIDEO

B Imagine the employees in a company have to agree on a new office space. What would their process be? How would it compare with the ants' process? Discuss your ideas in a small group.

CRITICAL THINKING: SYNTHESIZING

Writing

EXPLORING WRITTEN ENGLISH

LANGUAGE FOR WRITING Avoiding Plagiarism (I)—Paraphrasing

When you write a summary, it's important to paraphrase; that is, to use your own words. One method is to use synonyms for words that are in the original text.

~~Crowds~~ tend to be ~~wise~~ only if ~~individual~~ members ~~act responsibly~~ and make their own ~~decisions~~.

    Groups   *intelligent*   *single*   *behave appropriately*   *choices*

If you don't know a synonym for a word, you can use a thesaurus. However, it's important to make sure the synonym you choose matches the word in the context of your sentence. For example, *knowledgeable*, and *informed* are both synonyms for *wise*, but only *intelligent* works well in the context of the sentence above.

In addition to using synonyms, you can also change sentence structure and use different parts of speech. For example:

Only when single members behave appropriately and make their own choices, do groups tend to be intelligent.

A Choose the best synonym for each underlined word.

1. If one member of the group were to <u>break down</u>, others could take its place.

   a. explain   b. stop working   c. destroy

2. The robot <u>froze</u>, sending an image to its human supervisor.

   a. stopped   b. suspended   c. solidified

3. The research team <u>conducting</u> the experiment declared the run a success.

   a. behaving   b. passing through   c. performing

APPLYING   **B** Find a synonym for one other word or phrase in each of the sentences in exercise **A**. Then rewrite each sentence, changing the sentence structure and using different parts of speech when possible.

1. _____

   _____

   _____

2. _____

   _____

   _____

3. _____

   _____

WRITING SKILL Writing a Summary

When you write a summary, you report—in your own words—only the most important information from a passage in the same order that it is given in the original. A summary is shorter than the original passage. Follow these steps to summarize successfully.

1. Read the passage once. As you read, underline only the most important information. Then, without looking at it, write notes about the passage.

2. Reread the passage, comparing your notes against it to check your understanding. Correct any incorrect notes.

3. Use your notes to write a summary. Remember that the introductory statement in a summary is not quite the same as the thesis statement in a regular essay. The introductory statement is more like a restatement of the original author's main idea.

4. Compare your summary with the original. Make sure that your summary expresses the same meaning as the original.

5. Check your sentence structures and word choices. If your summary is very similar to the original, change your sentence structures and replace some content words (e.g., key nouns or noun phrases) with synonyms.

C Read the summaries of paragraph B of "The Smart Swarm." Answer the questions about the summaries below. With a partner, decide which summary is more successful. Why do you think so?

EVALUATING SUMMARIES

A According to Peter Miller, smart swarms are groups of individuals who react to their surroundings and each other and work together in order to make collective decisions. He explains that a group of birds is one example of a smart swarm. They fly to a location in a group, then fly away again in a coordinated manner.

B According to Peter Miller, a smart swarm is a group of people who work together as a group to deal with complex, uncertain things as well as change. He gives birds as an example of this. He watches flocks of pigeons in a park in Washington, D.C., and notices the way that birds move together as a group. They fly over cars and trees together and land at the same time on the ledges of buildings around the park. Then something disturbs them, and they take off again in a synchronized manner.

	A	B
1. Does the summary express the same meaning as the original?		
2. Does the summary include only important information from the original?		
3. Are the word choices different from those in the original?		
4. Are the sentence structures different from the structures in the original?		
5. Is the summary shorter than the original?		

WRITING TASK

GOAL You are going to write a summary essay on the following topic:

Write a summary of "The Smart Swarm."

BRAINSTORMING **A** Without looking back at the reading passage in this unit, write down the main ideas and details that you can remember. Share your ideas with a partner.

Author's main idea; what is one example of smart swarms?	
How can understanding smart swarms affect technology?	
How does swarm intelligence help animals?	
How do humans use swarm intelligence?	
What do individuals in human "smart swarms" have to do?	

TAKING NOTES **B** Look again at the reading passage in this unit. Compare the information with your notes from exercise **A** to check your understanding. Make any necessary corrections or additions.

VOCABULARY FOR WRITING **C** The words below can be useful when writing a summary. You can use these verbs to introduce an author's idea.

analyzes	argues	believes	calls for	claims
demands	discusses	disputes	examines	explains
explores	focuses on	mentions	provides	questions
recommends	reports	suggests	urges	wonders

Circle the correct word to complete the sentences below. Use a dictionary to help.

1. The writer **suggests / urges** us all to take immediate action on this critical issue.

2. Kolbert **discusses / calls for** the causes of deforestation in great depth.

3. The author **argues / disputes** some of the ideas put forward by other historians.

4. There has been decades of concern for tigers, but Alexander **mentions / questions** whether any progress has been made at all.

5. The writer **claims / provides** plentiful evidence to support her views on the topic.

D Follow the steps to make notes for your essay.

Step 1 Complete the introductory statement in the outline.

Step 2 Write the main questions that the author answers. Use these to organize the main points of your summary.

Step 3 For each body paragraph, write two or three examples or details that support your topic sentence.

Step 4 As a conclusion, write down Peter Miller's ideas for what he believes individuals in human "smart swarms" need to do.

OUTLINE

Introduction:

In "The Smart Swarm," author Peter Miller _____

_____

Body paragraph 1: What is a smart swarm?

Topic sentence: _____

_____

Details: _____

_____

_____

Body paragraph 2: _____?

Topic sentence: _____

_____

Details: _____

_____

_____

Body paragraph 3: _____?

Topic sentence: _____

Details: _____

_____

_____

Notes for conclusion: _____

_____

E Use the information in your outline to write a first draft of your essay.

REVISING PRACTICE

The draft below is a model of a summary essay. It summarizes the article "A Cry for the Tiger" from Unit 2. Follow the steps to create a better second draft.

Fix the following problems (1–3) with the essay.

1. Which two body paragraphs are in the wrong order?

2. Delete an unimportant detail in paragraph C.

3. Choose the best final sentence for the conclusion.

    a. According to the author, animal conservationists hope to work together to double the number of wild tigers in India within the next few years.

    b. The author calls on tiger conservationists to work extremely hard and to remain determined in order to save the tiger from extinction.

    c. The author believes that we need to act quickly because tiger populations are declining fast due to poaching and attacks by villagers.

A

In the article "A Cry for the Tiger," author Caroline Alexander argues that the beautiful and regal tiger is worth protecting, and that we need to find effective ways to keep it from disappearing.

B

According to Alexander, the tiger faces several threats. First, tigers are losing habitat because of quickly growing human populations. Second, this rapid population growth leads to poaching. Third, tiger parts are valuable in the black market. Finally, one of the least-discussed threats is the fact that strategies to protect tigers have been ineffective. In fact, experts estimated that there were about 8,000 tigers in the wild in the early 1980s. Now, decades later, there are fewer than 4,000.

C

Alexander reports that the countries that have wild tigers want to protect the animals, but it's difficult to find an effective solution. Right now, there are many tiger-conservation programs, and a lot of money is spent on tiger protection. For example, the Save the Tiger Fund gave more than $17 million in grants for tiger protection between 1995 and 2009. However, each program focuses on different strategies. Alexander argues that we need to spend our money and energy on four specific issues in order to protect tigers in the long run: core breeding populations, tiger reserves, wildlife corridors, and safety from poaching and killing. She believes that we have to prioritize these four issues, especially the protection of a core breeding population, and not spend money on things like eco-development and social programs.

D

Alexander explains that India is home to about 50 percent of the wild tiger population, and about one-third of these tigers live outside tiger reserves. In order for these tigers to survive in the wild, we need to ensure there are protected corridors of land between the safe areas. This way, the tigers outside of reserves can move freely without being killed by humans. Also, these corridors will allow tigers to mate and reproduce with tigers that live in different areas, resulting in greater genetic diversity. These corridors are necessary, but Alexander wonders if they are possible. Future infrastructure projects may make the creation of the corridors very difficult.

E

Is it possible not only to protect the remaining tigers but also to increase the wild tiger population? According to Alexander, most authorities believe that it is possible. But it won't be an easy fight. _____

F Now use the questions below to revise your essay.   REVISED DRAFT

☐ Have you paraphrased the language the author uses?
☐ Does your summary contain an introductory statement?
☐ Have you included any unnecessary details?
☐ Are your paragraphs in the correct order?
☐ Does your summary include the author's conclusion?

There are estimated to be fewer than 600 Siberian tigers left in the wild.

EDITING PRACTICE

Read the information below.

When you use synonyms, remember to make sure your synonym:
- has the same meaning as the original word.
- fits in the context of the sentence.

Find and correct one mistake with the underlined synonyms in each of the paraphrases below.

1. Original: What enables a <u>school</u> of herring to coordinate its movements so <u>precisely</u> it can change direction <u>in a flash</u> … ?

   Paraphrase: What enables a <u>group</u> of herring to coordinate its movements so <u>accurately</u> it can change direction <u>continuously</u> … ?

2. Original: <u>Within</u> five years, Kumar hopes to put a <u>networked</u> team of robotic vehicles <u>in the field</u>.

   Paraphrase: <u>In less than</u> five years, Kumar hopes to put a <u>connected</u> team of robotic vehicles <u>on the pitch</u>.

3. Original: When a predator <u>strikes</u> a school of fish, the group is capable of <u>scattering</u> in patterns that make it almost impossible to <u>track</u> any individual.

   Paraphrase: When a predator <u>attacks</u> a school of fish, the group is capable of <u>throwing</u> in patterns that make it almost impossible to <u>follow</u> any individual.

FINAL DRAFT **G** Follow the steps to write a final draft.

1. Check your revised draft for mistakes with paraphrasing.

2. Now use the checklist on page 248 to write a final draft. Make any other necessary changes.

UNIT REVIEW

Answer the following questions.

1. What are two examples of how humans can use swarm behavior?

_____

_____

2. What are two ways that ants collaborate?

_____

_____

3. Why is it important to paraphrase?

_____

_____

4. Do you remember the meanings of these words? Check (✓) the ones you know. Look back at the unit and review the ones you don't know.

☐ accomplish
☐ capability AWL
☐ collectively
☐ complementary AWL
☐ complex AWL
☐ coordinate AWL
☐ declare
☐ defense

☐ emergent AWL
☐ manipulate AWL
☐ precisely AWL
☐ realistically
☐ relevant AWL
☐ simulation
☐ unpredictable AWL

VOCABULARY EXTENSION   UNIT 1

WORD FORMS Adjectives Ending in -ic

For adjectives, the suffix -ic means "having the characteristics of." For example, *dramatic* means that something has the characteristics of a drama. To change an -ic adjective into an adverb, add -ally.

A Complete the chart. Use a dictionary to check your spelling.

Noun	Adjective	Adverb
academy		
	artistic	
athlete		
		atmospherically
	dramatic	
energy		
		linguistically

WORD PARTNERS *dramatic* + noun

Collocations are words that often go together. Here are some common collocations with the adjective *dramatic*.

dramatic **change**	dramatic **decline**
dramatic **increase**	dramatic **improvement**
dramatic **effect**	dramatic **action**
dramatic **moment**	dramatic **difference**

B Circle the best option to complete each sentence.

1. The world's governments need to take dramatic **action** / **change** to halt climate change.

2. The most dramatic **difference** / **moment** came towards the end of the movie.

3. Unfortunately, the past year has seen a dramatic **decline** / **increase** in our company's profits.

4. Studying philosophy had a dramatic **change** / **effect** on the way I thought about life.

5. There is a dramatic **difference** / **improvement** between the lives of the richest and poorest people on Earth.

VOCABULARY EXTENSION UNIT 2

Here are some adjectives that collocate with the noun *priority*.

high priority

low priority

first / **top** / **number one** priority

urgent / **immediate** priority

Below are some verbs that also collocate with *priority*. Read the definitions.

If you **give priority** to something, you make it the most important thing.

If you **identify priorities**, you decide on the most important things to do.

If one thing **takes priority** over another, it's more important.

A Circle the best option to complete each sentence.

1. Many parents tell their children that doing homework should **identify** / **take** priority over playing video games.

2. For most businesses, customer satisfaction is a **high** / **low** priority.

3. When boarding a plane, airlines often **give** / **take** priority to families with young children.

4. Before a hurricane strikes, evacuating residents in the hurricane's path is the **first** / **high** priority.

5. Compared to math and science, the teaching of arts is a **first** / **low** priority for many publicly-funded schools.

6. To manage your workload, **give** / **identify** priorities that are urgent versus ones that are less important.

7. As a parent, my **number one** / **low** priority in life is taking care of my son.

B Complete the sentences about yourself.

1. My number one priority in life is _____

_____.

2. For me, _____

takes priority over _____.

3. Next week, _____
is an urgent priority.

VOCABULARY EXTENSION   UNIT 3

WORD FORMS Nouns, Verbs, Adjectives, and Adverbs

Some words can be formed into nouns, verbs, adjectives, and adverbs. For example:
depression (noun), **depress** (verb), **depressing** (adjective), **depressingly** (adverb).

A Complete the chart below. Use a dictionary to check your answers.

Noun	Verb	Adjective	Adverbs
color		colorful	colorfully
depression	depress	depressing / depressed	depressingly
perfection		perfect	perfectly
proportion	proportion		proportionally
	satisfy	satisfactory	satisfactorily
style	style	stylish	

B Complete each sentence with one of the words in the chart above. More than one word may be possible.

1. Vincent Van Gogh's paintings are recognized for their bright, _____ palettes.

2. His earlier paintings were quite dark, but he developed a lighter, brighter _____ in his later work.

3. Van Gogh painted pictures of cypress trees. He remarked that the tall, thin shape of the trees gave them similar _____ to ancient Egyptian pillars.

4. Van Gogh was often _____ and spent several months in hospital for treatment.

5. *The Starry Night* is one of Van Gogh's most famous paintings. Many people think it _____ captures the bright night sky.

VOCABULARY EXTENSION   UNIT 4

WORD WEB Business Words and Antonyms

Profit and *loss* are antonyms. Below are other business words that have the opposite, or near opposite, meanings:

   shortage—surplus   *cash—credit*
   employer—employee   *revenue—expenditure*
   supply—demand   *high-end brand—low-end brand*

A Circle the best option to complete each sentence.

1. Gucci and Armani are examples of expensive, **high-end** / **low-end** clothing brands.

2. In economic theory, an increase in **demand** / **supply** for a product usually leads to an increase in prices.

3. Many companies reinvest their **profits** / **losses** to help their business grow.

4. A company is in financial difficulty if its **expenditure** / **revenue** exceeds its **expenditure** / **revenue**.

5. A **shortage** / **surplus** of crude oil usually leads to a rise in the price drivers pay at the gas pump.

WORD FORMS Adjectives with *-ive*

Many nouns ending in *-tion* can be made into adjectives using the suffix *-ive*. The suffix *-ive* means "having the quality of." For example, *competitive* means "having the quality of competition." Here are some other examples:

action	—	*active*	*definition*	—	*definitive*
competition	—	*competitive*	*destruction*	—	*destructive*
correction	—	*corrective*	*instruction*	—	*instructive*

B Complete each sentence with one of the nouns or adjectives in the box above.

1. In economics, a monopoly is a market where there is no _____.

2. The data that financial consultants provide to a business can be very _____.

3. The rise of online shopping has been _____ to many small and medium-sized stores that struggle to compete.

4. On learning that there was a serious fault in their new product, the company needed to decide quickly upon what _____ action to take.

5. During the 2008 financial crisis, many governments took prompt _____ to stabilize the financial markets.

VOCABULARY EXTENSION UNIT 5

WORD LINK co-, com-, col-

The prefixes *co-*, *com-*, and *col-* usually mean "with" or "together." For example, *cooperate* means to "work (or, operate) together."

A Match the words in **bold** (1–5) with the correct definitions (a–e).

1. At a party last night, I was wearing the exact same T-shirt as another guy. What a **coincidence**! _____

2. To make pancakes, **combine** eggs, flour, milk, and butter. Then heat the mixture in a pan. _____

3. Politicians and business leaders should **coordinate** to improve the conditions for workers. _____

4. There was heavy traffic yesterday following a **collision** between two vehicles. _____

5. The best meals have flavors, textures, and colors that **complement** each other. _____

a. to put together to make a whole

b. to go well together

c. to organize and work together in a systematic way

d. a situation where two similar events occur at the same time by chance

e. a situation where two or more objects crash into each other

B Circle the best option to complete each sentence. Use a dictionary to help.

1. My best friend owns a **collection** / **comparison** of rare postage stamps.

2. I recently **collaborated** / **combined** with my neighbors to start a fundraising project for local homeless people.

3. A quick **collection** / **comparison** of the two essays showed that it was a clear case of plagiarism.

4. The company's poor sales, **collaborated** / **combined** with its increased overheads, led to a terrible year financially.

Independent Student Handbook

TIPS FOR READING FLUENTLY

Reading slowly, one word at a time, makes it difficult to get an overall sense of the meaning of a text. As a result, reading becomes more challenging and less interesting. In general, it is a good idea to first skim a text for the gist, and then read it again more closely so that you can focus on the most relevant details. Use these strategies to improve your reading speed:

- Read groups of words rather than individual words.
- Keep your eyes moving forward. Read through to the end of each sentence or paragraph instead of going back to reread words or phrases.
- Skip functional words (articles, prepositions, etc.) and focus on words and phrases carrying meaning—the content words.
- Use clues in the text—such as **bold** words and words in *italics*—to help you know which parts might be important and worth focusing on.
- Use section headings, as well as the first and last lines of paragraphs, to help you understand how the text is organized.
- Use context clues, affixes, and parts of speech—instead of a dictionary—to guess the meaning of unfamiliar words and phrases.

TIPS FOR READING CRITICALLY

As you read, ask yourself questions about what the writer is saying, and how and why the writer is presenting the information at hand.

Important critical thinking skills for academic reading and writing:

- **Analyzing:** Examining a text in close detail in order to identify key points, similarities, and differences.

- **Applying:** Deciding how ideas or information might be relevant in a different context, e.g., applying possible solutions to problems.

- **Evaluating:** Using evidence to decide how relevant, important, or useful something is. This often involves looking at reasons for and against something.

- **Inferring:** "Reading between the lines"; in other words, identifying what a writer is saying indirectly, or *implicitly*, rather than directly, or *explicitly*.

- **Synthesizing:** Gathering appropriate information and ideas from more than one source and making a judgment, summary, or conclusion based on the evidence.

- **Reflecting:** Relating ideas and information in a text to your own personal experience and viewpoints.

TIPS FOR NOTE-TAKING

Taking notes will help you better understand the overall meaning and organization of a text. Note-taking also enables you to record the most important information for future uses— such as when you are preparing for an exam or completing a writing assignment. Use these techniques to make your note-taking more effective:

- As you read, underline or highlight important information such as dates, names, and places.

- Take notes in the margin. Note the main idea and supporting details next to each paragraph. Also note your own ideas or questions about the paragraph.

- On a separate piece of paper, write notes about the key points of the text in your own words. Include short headings, key words, page numbers, and quotations.

- Use a graphic organizer to summarize a text, particularly if it follows a pattern such as cause-effect, comparison-contrast, or chronological sequence.

- Keep your notes brief by using these abbreviations and symbols. Don't write full sentences.

approx.	approximately	→	leads to / causes
e.g./ex.	example	↑	increases / increased
i.e.	that is / in other words	↓	decreases / decreased
etc.	and others / and the rest	& or +	and
Ch.	Chapter	*b/c*	because
p. (pp.)	page (pages)	*w/*	with
re:	regarding, concerning	*w/o*	without
incl.	including	=	is the same as
excl.	excluding	>	is more than
info	information	<	is less than
yrs.	years	~	is approximately / about
para.	paragraph	∴	therefore

TIPS FOR LEARNING VOCABULARY

You often need to use a word or phrase several times before it enters your long-term memory. Here are some strategies for successfully learning vocabulary:

- Use flash cards to test your knowledge of new vocabulary. Write the word you want to learn on one side of an index card. Write the definition and/or an example sentence that uses the word on the other side.

- Use a vocabulary notebook to note down a new word or phrase. Write a short definition of the word in English and the sentence where you found it. Write another sentence of your own that uses the word. Include any common collocations (see *Word Partners* in the Vocabulary Extensions).

- Use memory aids, or mnemonics, to remember a word or phrase. For example, if you want to learn the idiom *keep an eye on someone*, which means "to watch someone carefully," you might picture yourself putting your eyeball on someone's shoulder so that you can watch the person carefully. The stranger the picture is, the more likely you will remember it!

- Make word webs or word maps. See the example below.

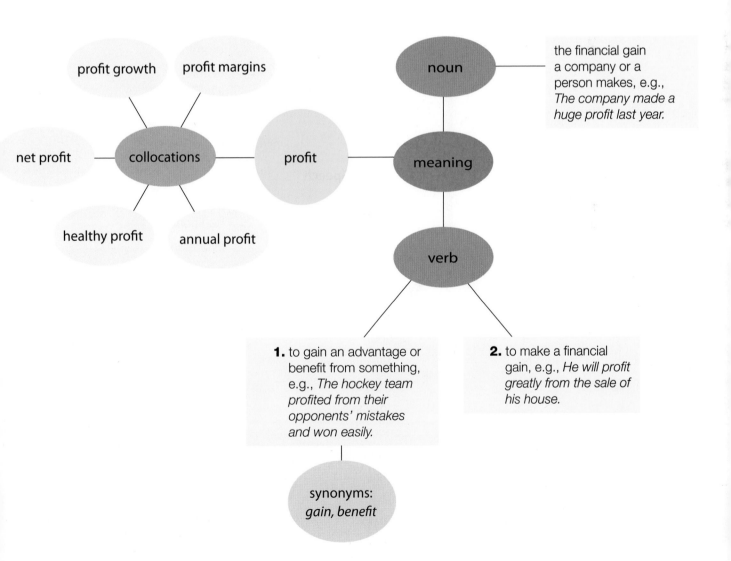

Common Affixes

Some words contain an affix at the start of the word (*prefix*) and/or at the end (*suffix*). These affixes can be useful for guessing the meaning of unfamiliar words and for expanding your vocabulary. In general, a prefix affects the meaning of a word, whereas a suffix affects its part of speech. See the examples below.

Prefix	Meaning	Example
com-	with	compile
con-	together, with	constitute
em- / en-	making, putting	empower, endanger
ex-	away, from, out	explode
im- / in-	not	imperfect, independent
inter-	between	interact
mis-	wrongly	mislead
mono-	one, only	monotonous
pre-	before	preview
pro-	forward, outward	prominent
re-	back, again	restore
trans-	across	transfer
un-	not	unclear
vid- / vis-	seeing	video, vision

Suffix	Part of Speech	Example
-able / -ible	adjective	affordable, feasible
-al	adjective	traditional
-ary	adjective	evolutionary
-ate	verb	generate
-ed	adjective	dedicated
-ent / -ant	adjective	confident, significant
-er	noun	researcher
-ful	adjective	harmful
-ic	adjective	nostalgic
-ical	adjective	hypothetical
-ism	noun	mechanism
-ity	noun	minority
-ive	adjective	inventive
-ize	verb	criticize
-ly	adverb	definitely
-ment	noun	replacement
-tion	noun	determination

TIPS FOR ACADEMIC WRITING

There are many types of academic writing (descriptive, argumentative/persuasive, narrative, etc.), but most types share similar characteristics. Generally, in academic writing, you should:

- write in full sentences.
- use formal English. (Avoid slang or conversational expressions such as *kind of*.)
- be clear and coherent—keep to your main point; avoid technical words that the reader may not know.
- use signal words or phrases and conjunctions to connect your ideas. (See examples below.)
- have a clear point (main idea) for each paragraph.
- use a neutral point of view—avoid overuse of personal pronouns (*I*, *we*, *you*) and subjective language such as *nice* or *terrible*.
- use facts, examples, and expert opinions to support your argument.
- avoid using abbreviations or language used in texting. (Use *that is* rather than *i.e.*, and *in my opinion*, not *IMO*.)
- avoid using contractions. (Use *is not* rather than *isn't*.)
- avoid starting sentences with *or*, *and*, or *but*.

Signal Words and Phrases

Use signal words and phrases to connect ideas and to make your writing more academic.

Giving personal opinions	Giving details and examples	Linking ideas
In my opinion, …	An example of this is …	Furthermore, …
I (generally) agree that …	Specifically, …	Moreover, …
I think/feel (that) …	For instance, …	In addition, …
I believe (that) …		Additionally, …
It is my personal view that …		
Presenting similar ideas	**Presenting contrasting views**	**Giving reasons**
Similarly, …	On the other hand, …	This is because (of) …
Both … and …	In contrast, …	This is due to …
Like … , …	Conversely, …	One reason (for this) is …
Likewise, …	Despite the fact that …	This is a consequence of …
	Even though …	
Describing effects	**Describing a process**	**Concluding**
Therefore, …	First (of all), …	In conclusion, …
As a result, …	Then / Next / After that, …	In summary, …
Because of this, …	As soon as …	To conclude, …
If … , then …	Once …	To summarize, …
	Finally, …	

Writing Citations

Below are some examples of how to cite print sources according to the American Psychological Association Style.

Guidelines	Reference entry	In-text citation
For an **article**, include the author's name, year and month of publication, article title, the name of the magazine/journal, and page references.	White, M. (2011, June). Brimming pools. *National Geographic*, 100–115.	(White, 2011) White (2011) says ...
For a **book**, include the author's name, year of publication, title of the book, the location of the publisher (if known), and the name of the publisher.	Hawking, S. (1988). *A brief history of time*. New York, NY: Bantam.	(Hawking, 1988) Hawking (1988) says ...
If there are **two authors**, use & to list their names.	Sherman, D., & Salisbury, J. (2008). *The west in the world: Renaissance to present*. New York, NY: McGraw-Hill.	(Sherman & Salisbury, 2008) Sherman and Salisbury (2008) say ...
For a **book that is not the first edition**, include the edition number after the title.	Turnbull, C. M. (2009). *A history of modern Singapore, 1819–2005*, (3rd ed.). Singapore: NUS Press.	(Turnbull, 2009) According to Turnbull (2009), ...

TIPS FOR EDITING

Capitalization

Remember to capitalize:

- the first letter of the word at the beginning of every sentence.

- proper nouns such as names of people, geographical names, company names, and names of organizations.

- days, months, and holidays.

- the word *I*.

- the first letter of a title such as the title of a movie or a book.

- the words in titles that have meaning (content words). Don't capitalize *a, an, the, and*, or prepositions such as *to, for, of, from, at, in,* and *on*, unless they are the first word of a title (e.g., *The Power of Creativity*).

Punctuation

- Use a period (.) at the end of any sentence that is not a question. Use a question mark (?) at the end of every question.

- Exclamation marks (!), which indicate strong feelings such as surprise or joy, are generally not used in academic writing.

- Use commas (,) to separate a list of three or more things. (*She speaks German, English, and Spanish.*)

- Use a comma after an introductory word or phrase. (*However, William didn't let that stop him.*)

- Use a comma before a combining word—*and, but, so, or*—that joins two sentences. (*Black widow spider bites are not usually deadly for adults, but they can be deadly for children.*)

- Use an apostrophe (') for showing possession. (*James's idea came from social networking websites.*)

- Use quotation marks (" ") to indicate the exact words used by someone else. (*"Our pleasures are really ancient," says psychologist Nancy Etcoff.*)

Other Proofreading Tips

- Print out your draft and read it out loud.

- Use a colored pen to make corrections on your draft so you can see them easily when you write your next draft.

- Have someone else read your draft and give you comments or ask you questions.

- Don't depend on a computer's spell-check. When the spell-check suggests a correction, make sure you agree with it before you accept the change.

- Check the spelling and accuracy of proper nouns, numbers, and dates.

- Keep a list of spelling and grammar mistakes that you commonly make so that you can be aware of them as you edit your draft.

- Check for frequently confused words:
  - *there, their*, and *they're*
  - *its* and *it's*
  - *your* and *you're*
  - *then* and *than*
  - *to, too*, and *two*
  - *whose* and *who's*
  - *where, wear, we're*, and *were*
  - *affect* and *effect*

EDITING CHECKLIST

Use the checklist to find errors in the second draft of your writing task for each unit.

	Unit				
	1	2	3	4	5
1. Did you use capitalization correctly, e.g., for the first word of a sentence, for proper nouns, etc.					
2. Do your subjects and verbs agree?					
3. Are commas and other punctuation marks used correctly?					
4. Have you used an appropriate level of formality?					
5. Is the spelling of places, people, and other proper nouns correct?					
6. Did you check for frequently confused words? (see examples in the *Tips for Editing* section)					
7. Did you use appropriate signal words and phrases to introduce and connect ideas? (see examples in the *Tips for Academic Writing* section)					
8. For essays that require research and the use of information from external sources, did you cite all sources properly? (see examples in the *Writing Citations* section)					

WRITING REFERENCE

UNIT 3

Restrictive and Nonrestrictive Adjective Clauses

There are two types of adjective clauses. One type gives essential information about the noun. These are called **restrictive adjective clauses**. Do not use commas with restrictive adjective clauses.	I saw a photograph **that** illustrated all of Griffiths's aesthetic principles. I read the essay on photography **that** Annie Griffiths wrote.
The other type of adjective clause gives extra, or nonessential, information about the noun. These are called **nonrestrictive adjective clauses.** Commas always set off nonrestrictive adjective clauses.	Photography, **which** is a relatively recent invention, influenced our notions of beauty. Susan Sontag, **who** was a noted essayist, wrote a book on photography. Japonaiserie, **which** is also referred to as Japonism, is an artistic movement from the mid-1800s. Vincent van Gogh, **who/whom** many people consider one of the greatest Impressionists, was influenced by Japanese woodblock prints.

UNIT 4

Initial Phrases

You can use initial phrases (prepositional, time, and verbal phrases) to avoid short, choppy sentences. Using initial phrases is also a way to vary your sentence style and to show the relationship between ideas.

Prepositional phrases	**In Africa**, Nigeria is the most populous country. **At a distance of 4.3 light-years**, Alpha Centauri is the nearest star outside our Solar System. **Just opposite this building**, you can find a really good restaurant.
Time phrases	**Since I was a young child**, I've had a keen interest in science. **When she first started the business**, there were many problems to deal with. **Once I met her**, I realized why she'd been so successful in life.
Verbal phrases	**Starting in Peru**, the Amazon River runs through seven separate countries. **Concerned about the increasing workload**, he decided to look for a new job. **Painted by Leonardo da Vinci**, the *Mona Lisa* is one of the most valuable paintings in the world.

Inversion with Negative Adverb Phrases

In formal writing, when certain negative adverb phrases are used at the start of a sentence, the subject and auxiliary verb of the main clause must be inverted (switched). Look at the examples on the right.	**Never before** <u>have I</u> found a book so difficult to put down. **Not since** I went to New Zealand <u>have I</u> seen such amazing scenery. **Not until** I arrived at the shop <u>did I</u> realize I'd forgotten my wallet.

WRITING REFERENCE

UNIT 5

Paraphrasing

When you want to report what someone else wrote, but you don't want to quote the person directly, you can paraphrase. Paraphrasing is using your own words to express another person's idea. Paraphrasing is different from summarizing. For example, when you summarize a paragraph, you restate the main points of the paragraph. When you paraphrase a paragraph, you restate all of the ideas of the paragraph.

Follow these steps to help you paraphrase successfully:

1. Read the original passage that you want to paraphrase several times to make sure that you understand the meaning. Look up any words that you don't understand.

2. Without looking at the original passage, write notes about it on a piece of paper. Don't write complete sentences.

3. Use your notes to write a paraphrase. Don't look at the original passage.

4. Compare your paraphrase with the original passage. Make sure that your paraphrase expresses the same meaning as the original. If your paraphrase looks too much like the original, check your sentence structures and word choices. Make sure that your sentence structures are different from the original. Also, try to use synonyms for the content words (like nouns and verbs) in the original passage.

Here's an example of a paraphrase:

Original Passage:

Between 1960 and 2000, Seoul's population increased from fewer than three million to almost ten million people. In the same period, South Korea went from being one of the world's poorest countries, with a per capita GDP of less than $100, to being richer than some countries in Europe.

Paraphrase:

The population of Seoul grew a lot between 1960 and 2000. In 1960, there were fewer than three million people in Seoul. By 2000, just under 10 million people were living there. In 1960, the per capita GDP of South Korea was less than $100, and the country was one of the poorest in the world. However, by 2000, South Korea was wealthier than some European countries.

VOCABULARY INDEX

Word	Unit	CEFR	Example sentence / definition
accomplish	5	C1	
acknowledge*	2	C1	
alien	10	-	
annual*	7	B1	
apparel	4	-	
apparently*	2	B2	
assess*	2	B2	
associate (v)	7	C1	
atmosphere	1	B2	
authority*	2	C2	
automatically*	9	B2	
balance (n)	3	B2	
base (n)	10	C2	
beyond	8	B2	
brand	4	B2	
capability*	5	C1	
capacity*	9	B2	
captivated	6	-	
collectively	5	-	
competitive	4	B2	
competitor	4	B1	
complementary*	5	-	
complex* (adj)	5	B2	
composition	3	C2	
concept*	1	B2	

Target vocabulary items in this split edition are in blue.

Word	Unit	CEFR	Example sentence / definition
consequence*	1	B2	_____
context*	3	B2	_____
contradictory*	8	C2	_____
conversely*	8	-	_____
coordinate*	5	-	_____
cover up	9	C1	_____
criteria*	1	C1	_____
crops	7	B1	_____
crucial*	3	B2	_____
cryptic	6	-	_____
current	1	B2	_____
deceitful	9	-	_____
deceptive	9	C2	_____
declare	5	B2	_____
dedicated*	2	C1	_____
defense	5	-	_____
definitively*	6	-	_____
deny*	7	B2	_____
depression*	3	B2	_____
destiny	10	C1	_____
devoted to*	1	B2	_____
distinct*	7	C1	_____
dramatic*	1	B2	_____
economic*	7	B2	_____
eliminate*	1	C1	_____

Word	Unit	CEFR	Example sentence / definition
emergence*	9	-	_____
emergent*	5	-	_____
erosion*	1	C1	_____
essentially	1	B2	_____
ethics*	3	C2	_____
evidently*	6	B2	_____
evolutionary*	7	-	_____
exclude*	6	C1	_____
executive	4	C1	_____
expose to*	3	B2	_____
feasible	2	C1	_____
fertilizer	1	-	_____
flee	10	C1	_____
found*	4	B2	_____
fundamental*	9	C2	_____
gain insight*	8	C1	_____
geometric	3	-	_____
glimpse	10	C1	_____
gullible	9	-	_____
headquarters	4	B2	_____
hypothetical*	2	-	_____
imperfect	3	C1	_____
implication*	8	C1	_____
impostor*	9	-	_____
inferior	10	C1	_____

Word	Unit	CEFR	Example sentence / definition
innocence	9	C2	_____
insight*	3	C1	_____
intact	8	C2	_____
integral*	6	C1	_____
intellectual	10	B2	_____
investment*	7	B2	_____
irresistible	6	-	_____
lethal	2	C2	_____
life span	8	C2	_____
literally	10	B2	_____
livestock	7	-	_____
longevity	8	C2	_____
manipulate*	5	-	_____
marketing	4	B2	_____
mechanisms*	8	C1	_____
merchandise	4	-	_____
metaphor	6	C2	_____
minority	7	B2	_____
mislead	9	C1	_____
monotonous	6	C1	_____
multiple	6	C1	_____
nostalgic	6	C2	_____
notion*	3	C1	_____
on the contrary*	6	C1	_____
orientation*	7	C2	_____

Word	Unit	CEFR	Example sentence / definition
outcome*	8	C1	
outnumber	8	C1	
outsource	4	-	
perspective*	1	C1	
poaching	2	-	
precisely*	5	B2	
predator	2	C1	
prey	2	C2	
principle*	3	C1	
priority*	2	B2	
profit	4	B2	
profound	1	C2	
project* (v)	2	-	
prominent	9	C1	
prone to	9	C2	
proportion*	3	C1	
prosper	7	C2	
protagonist	10	C2	
pursue*	3	C1	
ratio*	8	C1	
realistically*	5	C1	
reconstruct*	8	C1	
relevant*	5	B2	
resolve*	2	C1	
restriction*	8	C1	

Word	Unit	CEFR	Example sentence / definition
retail	4	C1	_____
revenue*	7	C1	_____
rival	4	C1	_____
ruthless	10	C2	_____
satisfy	1	B2	_____
secretive	2	-	_____
sequel	10	-	_____
settle	10	B2	_____
shortage	4	B2	_____
simulation*	5	C1	_____
simultaneously	6	B2	_____
straightforward*	6	B2	_____
stunned	10	C2	_____
substantial	6	B2	_____
supply chain	4	-	_____
systematically	9	C2	_____
tensions*	7	B2	_____
thereby*	7	C1	_____
thrive	9	C1	_____
touch down	10	-	_____
transform*	1	B2	_____
undermine	8	C2	_____
unimaginable	10	C2	_____
unpredictable*	5	B2	_____
violate*	3	C2	_____

*These words are on the Academic Word List (AWL). The AWL is a list of the 570 most frequent word families in academic texts. It does not include the most frequent 2,000 words of English.

ACKNOWLEDGMENTS

The Authors and Publisher would like to acknowledge the teachers around the world who participated in the development of the second edition of *Pathways*.

A special thanks to our Advisory Board for their valuable input during the development of this series.

ADVISORY BOARD

Mahmoud Al Hosni, Modern College of Business and Science, Oman; **Safaa Al-Salim**, Kuwait University; **Laila Al-Qadhi**, Kuwait University; **Julie Bird**, RMIT University Vietnam; **Elizabeth Bowles**, Virginia Tech Language and Culture Institute, Blacksburg, VA; **Rachel Bricker**, Arizona State University, Tempe, AZ; **James Broadbridge**, J.F. Oberlin University, Tokyo; **Marina Broeder**, Mission College, Santa Clara, CA; **Shawn Campbell**, Hangzhou High School; **Trevor Carty**, James Cook University, Singapore; **Jindarat De Vleeschauwer**, Chiang Mai University; **Wai-Si El Hassan**, Prince Mohammad Bin Fahd University, Saudi Arabia; **Jennifer Farnell**, University of Bridgeport, Bridgeport, CT; **Rasha Gazzaz**, King Abdulaziz University, Saudi Arabia; **Keith Graziadei**, Santa Monica College, Santa Monica, CA; **Janet Harclerode**, Santa Monica Community College, Santa Monica, CA; **Anna Hasper**, TeacherTrain, UAE; **Phoebe Kamel Yacob Hindi**, Abu Dhabi Vocational Education and Training Institute, UAE; **Kuei-ping Hsu**, National Tsing Hua University; **Greg Jewell**, Drexel University, Philadelphia, PA; **Adisra Katib**, Chulalongkorn University Language Institute, Bangkok; **Wayne Kennedy**, LaGuardia Community College, Long Island City, NY; **Beth Koo**, Central Piedmont Community College, Charlotte, NC; **Denise Kray**, Bridge School, Denver, CO; **Chantal Kruger**, ILA Vietnam; **William P. Kyzner**, Fuyang AP Center; **Becky Lawrence**, Massachusetts International Academy, Marlborough, MA; **Deborah McGraw**, Syracuse University, NY; **Mary Moore**, University of Puerto Rico; **Raymond Purdy**, ELS Language Centers, Princeton, NJ; **Anouchka Rachelson**, Miami Dade College, Miami, FL; **Fathimah Razman**, Universiti Utara Malaysia; **Phil Rice**, University of Delaware ELI, Newark, DE; **Scott Rousseau**, American University of Sharjah, UAE; **Verna Santos-Nafrada**, King Saud University, Saudi Arabia; **Eugene Sidwell**, American Intercon Institute, Phnom Penh; **Gemma Thorp**, Monash University English Language Centre, Australia; **Matt Thurston**, University of Central Lancashire, UK; **Christine Tierney**, Houston Community College, Houston, TX; **Jet Robredillo Tonogbanua**, FPT University, Hanoi.

GLOBAL REVIEWERS

ASIA

Antonia Cavcic, Asia University, Tokyo; **Soyhan Egitim**, Tokyo University of Science; **Caroline Handley**, Asia University, Tokyo; **Patrizia Hayashi**, Meikai University, Urayasu; **Greg Holloway**, University of Kitakyushu; **Anne C. Ihata**, Musashino University, Tokyo; **Kathryn Mabe**, Asia University, Tokyo; **Frederick Navarro Bacala**, Yokohama City University; **Tyson Rode**, Meikai University, Urayasu; **Scott Shelton-Strong**, Asia University, Tokyo; **Brooks Slaybaugh**, Yokohama City University; **Susanto Sugiharto**, Sutomo Senior High School, Medan; **Andrew Zitzmann**, University of Kitakyushu.

LATIN AMERICA AND THE CARIBBEAN

Raul Bilini, ProLingua, Dominican Republic; **Alejandro Garcia**, Colegio Marcelina, Mexico; **Humberto Guevara**, Tec de Monterrey, Campus Monterrey, Mexico; **Romina Olga Planas**, Centro Cultural Paraguayo Americano, Paraguay; **Carlos Rico-Troncoso**, Pontificia Universidad Javeriana, Colombia; **Ialê Schetty**, Enjoy English, Brazil; **Aline Simoes**, Way To Go Private English, Brazil; **Paulo Cezar Lira Torres**, APenglish, Brazil; **Rosa Enilda Vasquez**, Swisher Dominicana, Dominican Republic; **Terry Whitty**, LDN Language School, Brazil.

MIDDLE EAST AND NORTH AFRICA

Susan Daniels, Kuwait University, Kuwait; **Mahmoud Mohammadi Khomeini**, Sokhane Ashna Language School, Iran; **Müge Lenbet**, Koç University, Turkey; **Robert Anthony Lowman**, Prince Mohammad bin Fahd University, Saudi Arabia; **Simon Mackay**, Prince Mohammad bin Fahd University, Saudi Arabia.

USA AND CANADA

Frank Abbot, Houston Community College, Houston, TX; **Hossein Aksari**, Bilingual Education Institute and Houston Community College, Houston, TX; **Sudie Allen-Henn**, North Seattle College, Seattle, WA; **Sharon Allie**, Santa Monica Community College, Santa Monica, CA; **Jerry Archer**, Oregon State University, Corvallis, OR; **Nicole Ashton**, Central Piedmont Community College, Charlotte, NC; **Barbara Barrett**, University of Miami, Coral Gables, FL; **Maria Bazan-Myrick**, Houston Community College, Houston, TX; **Rebecca Beal**, Colleges of Marin, Kentfield, CA; **Marlene Beck**, Eastern Michigan University, Ypsilanti, MI; **Michelle Bell**, University of Southern California, Los Angeles, CA; **Linda Bolet**, Houston Community College, Houston, TX; **Jenna Bollinger**, Eastern Michigan University, Ypsilanti, MI; **Monica Boney**, Houston Community College, Houston, TX; **Nanette Bouvier**, Rutgers University – Newark, Newark, NJ; **Nancy Boyer**, Golden West College, Huntington Beach, CA; **Lia Brenneman**, University of Florida English Language Institute, Gainesville, FL; **Colleen Brice**, Grand Valley State University, Allendale, MI; **Kristen Brown**, Massachusetts International Academy, Marlborough, MA; **Philip Brown**, Houston Community College, Houston, TX; **Dongmei Cao**, San Jose City College, San Jose, CA; **Molly Cheney**, University of Washington, Seattle, WA; **Emily Clark**, The University of Kansas, Lawrence, KS; **Luke Coffelt**, International English Center, Boulder, CO; **William C. Cole-French**, MCPHS University,

Boston, MA; **Charles Colson**, English Language Institute at Sam Houston State University, Huntsville, TX; **Lucy Condon**, Bilingual Education Institute, Houston, TX; **Janice Crouch**, Internexus Indiana, Indianapolis, IN; **Charlene Dandrow**, Virginia Tech Language and Culture Institute, Blacksburg, VA; **Loretta Davis**, Coastline Community College, Westminster, CA; **Marta Dmytrenko-Ahrabian**, Wayne State University, Detroit, MI; **Bonnie Duhart**, Houston Community College, Houston, TX; **Karen Eichhorn**, International English Center, Boulder, CO; **Tracey Ellis**, Santa Monica Community College, Santa Monica, CA; **Jennifer Evans**, University of Washington, Seattle, WA; **Marla Ewart**, Bilingual Education Institute, Houston, TX; **Rhoda Fagerland**, St. Cloud State University, St. Cloud, MN; **Kelly Montijo Fink**, Kirkwood Community College, Cedar Rapids, IA; **Celeste Flowers**, University of Central Arkansas, Conway, AR; **Kurtis Foster**, Missouri State University, Springfield, MO; **Rachel Garcia**, Bilingual Education Institute, Houston, TX; **Thomas Germain**, University of Colorado Boulder, Boulder, CO; **Claire Gimble**, Virginia International University, Fairfax, VA; **Marilyn Glazer-Weisner**, Middlesex Community College, Lowell, MA; **Amber Goodall**, South Piedmont Community College, Charlotte, NC; **Katya Goussakova**, Seminole State College of Florida, Sanford, FL; **Jane Granado**, Texas State University, San Marcos, TX; **Therea Hampton**, Mercer County Community College, West Windsor Township, NJ; **Jane Hanson**, University of Nebraska – Lincoln, Lincoln, NE; **Lauren Heather**, University of Texas at San Antonio, San Antonio, TX; **Jannette Hermina**, Saginaw Valley State University, Saginaw, MI; **Gail Hernandez**, College of Staten Island, Staten Island, NY; **Beverly Hobbs**, Clark University, Worcester, MA; **Kristin Homuth**, Language Center International, Southfield, MI; **Tim Hooker**, Campbellsville University, Campbellsville, KY; **Raylene Houck**, Idaho State University, Pocatello, ID; **Karen L. Howling**, University of Bridgeport, Bridgeport, CT; **Sharon Jaffe**, Santa Monica Community College, Santa Monica, CA; **Andrea Kahn**, Santa Monica Community College, Santa Monica, CA; **Eden Bradshaw Kaiser**, Massachusetts International Academy, Marlborough, MA; **Mandy Kama**, Georgetown University, Washington, D.C.; **Andrea Kaminski**, University of Michigan – Dearborn, Dearborn, MI; **Eileen Kramer**, Boston University CELOP, Brookline, MA; **Rachel Lachance**, University of New Hampshire, Durham, NH; **Janet Langon**, Glendale Community College, Glendale, CA; **Frances Le Grand**, University of Houston, Houston, TX; **Esther Lee**, California State University, Fullerton, CA; **Helen S. Mays Lefal**, American Learning Institute, Dallas, TX; **Oranit Limmaneeprasert**, American River College, Sacramento, CA; **Dhammika Liyanage**, Bilingual Education Institute, Houston, TX; **Emily Lodmer**, Santa Monica Community College, Santa Monica, CA; **Ari Lopez**, American Learning Institute, Dallas, TX; **Nichole Lukas**, University of Dayton, Dayton, OH; **Undarmaa Maamuujav**, California State University, Los Angeles, CA; **Diane Mahin**, University of Miami, Coral Gables, FL; **Melanie Majeski**, Naugatuck Valley Community College, Waterbury, CT; **Judy Marasco**, Santa Monica Community College, Santa Monica, CA; **Murray McMahan**, University of Alberta, Edmonton, AB, Canada; **Deirdre McMurtry**, University of Nebraska Omaha, Omaha, NE; **Suzanne Meyer**, University of Pittsburgh, Pittsburgh, PA; **Cynthia Miller**, Richland College, Dallas, TX; **Sara Miller**, Houston Community College, Houston, TX; **Gwendolyn Miraglia**, Houston Community College, Houston, TX; **Katie Mitchell**, International English Center, Boulder, CO; **Ruth Williams Moore**, University of Colorado Boulder, Boulder, CO; **Kathy Najafi**, Houston Community College, Houston, TX; **Sandra Navarro**, Glendale Community College, Glendale, CA; **Stephanie Ngom**, Boston University, Boston, MA; **Barbara Niemczyk**, University of Bridgeport, Bridgeport, CT; **Melody Nightingale**, Santa Monica Community College, Santa Monica, CA; **Alissa Olgun**, California Language Academy, Los Angeles, CA; **Kimberly Oliver**, Austin Community College, Austin, TX; **Steven Olson**, International English Center, Boulder, CO; **Fernanda Ortiz**, University of Arizona, Tucson, AZ; **Joel Ozretich**, University of Washington, Seattle, WA; **Erin Pak**, Schoolcraft College, Livonia, MI; **Geri Pappas**, University of Michigan – Dearborn, Dearborn, MI; **Eleanor Paterson**, Erie Community College, Buffalo, NY; **Sumeeta Patnaik**, Marshall University, Huntington, WV; **Mary Peacock**, Richland College, Dallas, TX; **Kathryn Porter**, University of Houston, Houston, TX; **Eileen Prince**, Prince Language Associates, Newton Highlands, MA; **Marina Ramirez**, Houston Community College, Houston, TX; **Laura Ramm**, Michigan State University, East Lansing, MI; **Chi Rehg**, University of South Florida, Tampa, FL; **Cyndy Reimer**, Douglas College, New Westminster, BC, Canada; **Sydney Rice**, Imperial Valley College, Imperial, CA; **Lynnette Robson**, Mercer University, Macon, GA; **Helen E. Roland**, Miami Dade College, Miami, FL; **Maria Paula Carreira Rolim**, Southeast Missouri State University, Cape Girardeau, MO; **Jill Rolston-Yates**, Texas State University, San Marcos, TX; **David Ross**, Houston Community College, Houston, TX; **Rachel Scheiner**, Seattle Central College, Seattle, WA; **John Schmidt**, Texas Intensive English Program, Austin, TX; **Mariah Schueman**, University of Miami, Coral Gables, FL; **Erika Shadburne**, Austin Community College, Austin, TX; **Mahdi Shamsi**, Houston Community College, Houston, TX; **Osha Sky**, Highline College, Des Moines, WA; **William Slade**, University of Texas, Austin, TX; **Takako Smith**, University of Nebraska – Lincoln, Lincoln, NE; **Barbara Smith-Palinkas**, Hillsborough Community College, Tampa, FL; **Paula Snyder**, University of Missouri, Columbia, MO; **Mary Evelyn Sorrell**, Bilingual Education Institute, Houston, TX; **Kristen Stauffer**, International English Center, Boulder, CO; **Christina Stefanik**, The Language Company, Toledo, OH; **Cory Stewart**, University of Houston, Houston, TX; **Laurie Stusser-McNeill**, Highline College, Des Moines, WA; **Tom Sugawara**, University of Washington, Seattle, WA; **Sara Sulko**, University of Missouri, Columbia, MO; **Mark Sullivan**, University of Colorado Boulder, Boulder, CO; **Olivia Szabo**, Boston University, Boston, MA; **Amber Tallent**, University of Nebraska Omaha, Omaha, NE; **Amy Tate**, Rice University, Houston, TX; **Aya C. Tiacoh**, Bilingual Education Institute, Houston, TX; **Troy Tucker**, Florida SouthWestern State College, Fort Myers, FL; **Anne Tyoan**, Savannah College of Art and Design, Savannah, GA; **Michael Vallee**, International English Center, Boulder, CO; **Andrea Vasquez**, University of Southern Maine, Portland, ME; **Jose Vasquez**, University of Texas Rio Grande Valley, Edinburg, TX; **Maureen Vendeville**, Savannah Technical College, Savannah, GA; **Melissa Vervinck**, Oakland University, Rochester, MI; **Adriana Villarreal**, Universidad Nacional Autonoma de Mexico, San Antonio, TX; **Summer Webb**, International English Center, Boulder, CO; **Mercedes Wilson-Everett**, Houston Community College, Houston, TX; **Lora Yasen**, Tokyo International University of America, Salem, OR; **Dennis Yommer**, Youngstown State University, Youngstown, OH; **Melojeane (Jolene) Zawilinski**, University of Michigan – Flint, Flint, MI.

CREDITS

Photos

Cover, iii Robbie Shone/National Geographic Creative, **iv** (from top to bottom) © Edward Burtynsky, Michael Nichols/National Geographic Creative, Francois Nel/Getty Images, View Pictures/UIG/Getty Images, Matthias Hangst/Getty Images, **1** © Edward Burtynsky, **2** sunlow/Getty Images, **3** (tl) Chris Gray/National Geographic Creative, (tr) Robytravel/Alamy Stock Photo, **4** Xinhua News Agency/Getty Images, **6** Paul Chesley/National Geographic Creative, **9** © Edward Burtynsky, **10–11** (spread) Jim Richardson/National Geographic Creative, **11** (br) © Nicholas Whitman, **13** National Geographic Creative, **16** Frans Lanting/National Geographic Creative, **18–19** (spread) National Geographic Creative, **23** National Geographic Creative, **25** Michael Nichols/National Geographic Creative, **26** Janette Hill/National Geographic Creative, **27** (cr) (bl) (tl) Joel Sartore/National Geographic Creative, **28** James R.D. Scott/Getty Images, **30** Steve Winter/National Geographic Creative, **32** Steve Winter/National Geographic Creative, **34** (b) Steve Winter/National Geographic Creative, (cr) Evan Agostini/Getty Images, **38** Konrad Wothe/Minden Pictures, **40** Joel Sartore/National Geographic Creative, **42** Dmitrij Skorobogatov/Shutterstock, **45** National Geographic Creative, **47** Francois Nel/Getty Images, **48–49** (spread) FineArt/Alamy Stock Photo, **50** (bl) Bridgeman Images, (br) Interfoto/Alamy Stock Photo, **52** Raymond Gehman/National Geographic Creative, **54** Sam Abell/National Geographic Creative, **55** James L. Stanfield/National Geographic Creative, **56** Michael Melford/National Geographic Creative, **57** (t) Annie Griffiths/National Geographic Creative, (br) Araya Diaz/Getty Images, **59** O. Louis Mazzatenta/National Geographic Image Collection, **61** © Brian Yen, **66** Richard Nowitz/National Geographic Creative, **71** View Pictures/UIG/Getty Images, **72–73** (spread) National Geographic Creative, **72** (bl) Richard Boll/Getty Images, **74** (b) AP Images/Lee Jin-man, **76** Newscast/Eyevine/Redux, **78–79** (spread) Xurxo Lobato/Getty Images, **80** (tr) © Mike Peng, (bl) Jock Fistick/Bloomberg via Getty Images, **83** Miguel Riopa/Getty Images, **84** Christopher Goodney/Bloomberg/Getty Images, **93** Matthias Hangst/Getty Images, **94–95** (spread) David Ramos/Getty Images, **98** Frans Lanting/National Geographic Creative, **100** Mauricio Handler/National Geographic Creative, **101** Mark Thiessen/National Geographic Creative, **102–103** (spread) Kenneth Whitten/Design Pics/National Geographic Creative, **103** (br) © Peter Miller, **108** Anand Varma/National Geographic Creative, **114–115** (spread) Kathleen Reeder Wildlife Photography/Getty Images, **241** Jim Richardson/National Geographic Creative

Texts/Sources

6–11 Adapted from "The Age of Man," by Elizabeth Kolbert: NGM March 2011; **30–34** Adapted from "A Cry for the Tiger," by Caroline Alexander: NGM December 2011; **52–57** Adapted from the Introduction to *Simply Beautiful Photographs* pp. 25–31, by Annie Griffiths: National Geographic Books, 2010; **72–73** Based on information from "Global Fashion Industry Statistics": www.fashionunited.com; "The World's Largest Apparel Companies 2016": www.forbes.com; "Who Spends the Most on Apparel": www.wwd.com; "The Impact of a Cotton T-Shirt": www.worldwildlife.org; **76–80** Adapted from "Zara Excels in Marketing and Supply Chain Management," by Mike W. Peng: *Global Business 4th Edition* © Cengage Learning 2015; **98–103** Adapted from "Swarm Theory," by Peter Miller: NGM July 2007

NGM = National Geographic Magazine

Maps and Infographics

2–3 National Geographic Maps; **33** Virginia W Mason/National Geographic Creative; **72** 5W Infographics

INDEX OF EXAM SKILLS AND TASKS

The activities in *Pathways Reading, Writing, and Critical Thinking* develop **key reading skills** needed for success on standardized tests such as TOEFL® and IELTS. In addition, many of the activities provide useful exam practice because they are similar to **common question types** in these tests.

Key Reading Skills	IELTS	TOEFL®	Page(s)
Recognizing vocabulary from context	✓	✓	14, 17, 18, 26, 36, 39, 59, 62, 63, 81, 85, 104, 109, 127, 130, 154, 155, 176, 179, 196, 200, 219, 223
Identifying main ideas	✓	✓	12, 35, 58, 81, 104, 126, 150, 175, 196, 219
Identifying supporting ideas	✓	✓	12, 35, 58, 81, 104, 126, 150, 175, 176, 196, 219, 220, 221
Scanning for details	✓	✓	12, 35, 82, 105, 126, 151, 196, 219
Making inferences	✓	✓	39, 85, 127, 168, 221
Recognizing pronoun references	✓	✓	15, 19
Understanding charts and infographics	✓		2, 13, 72, 82, 118, 140, 164, 177, 178, 188, 201, 202, 208

Common Question Types	IELTS	TOEFL®	Page(s)
Multiple choice	✓	✓	20, 39, 75, 81, 83, 110, 154, 177, 179, 211, 223
Completion (notes, diagram, chart)	✓		13, 14, 17, 35, 60, 82, 105, 154, 176, 200
Completion (summary)	✓		150, 196
Short answer	✓		12, 39, 58, 85, 106, 109, 126, 151, 175, 219, 220, 221, 223
Matching headings / information	✓		35, 36, 62, 104, 106, 126, 128, 218
Categorizing (Matching features)	✓	✓	62, 132, 150, 154, 219
True / False / Not Given	✓		17
Prose summary		✓	110, 111
Rhetorical purpose		✓	126, 127, 152, 220, 221

Level 4 of *Pathways Reading, Writing, and Critical Thinking* also develops **key writing skills** needed for exam success.

Key Writing Skills	Unit(s)
Writing a strong introduction and conclusion	1, 2
Expressing and justifying opinions	1, 2, 3, 6, 8, 10
Giving reasons and examples	1, 2, 3, 4, 6, 7, 8, 9, 10
Paraphrasing / Summarizing	4, 5, 7, 9, 10
Making comparisons	4
Describing problems and solutions	1, 2, 8
Explaining a process	9
Expressing agreement and disagreement	3, 8
Describing a graph or chart	9

Pathways	CEFR	IELTS Band	TOEFL® Score
Level 4	**C1**	**6.5–7.0**	**81–100**
Level 3	B2	5.5–6.0	51–80
Level 2	B1–B2	4.5–5.0	31–50
Level 1	A2–B1	0–4.0	0–30
Foundations	A1–A2		